Excel 2021

The Step By Step Guide to Learn Everything That You Need To Know About Microsoft Excel 2021

DARREN SHEPHERD

Respective authors own all copyrights not held by the publisher.

The information herein is offered for informational purposes solely and is universal as such. The presentation of the information is without a contract or any guarantee assurance.

The trademarks used are without any consent, and the publication of the trademark is without permission or backing by the trademark owner. All trademarks and brands within this book are for clarifying purposes only and are owned by the owners themselves, not affiliated with this document.

Table of Content

Introduction

Microsoft Excel is spreadsheet software that lets you organize, record, evaluate, track, and analyze almost every kind of data. It's part of the Microsoft Office family of products.

Excel allows users to generate anything from quick collections and basic arithmetic formulas, as well as interact with external sources and analyse millions of documents. In milliseconds, complex engineering equations and statistics may be done. Repeated spreadsheet operations may be streamlined and completed with a simple mouse click.

You can quickly produce professional-looking budgets, surveys, forecasts, invoices, tables, maps, matrices, and practically every other kind of artefact containing language, money, numeric, or time values using formatting, graphs, and other presentation methods.

Excel is also the technology in the Microsoft Office suite that interacts the most with other applications. For instance, if you had consumer and sales details in Excel, you might export it to Word and build client invoices.

For research, testing, project plans, and more, you can conveniently import data from Access or a variety of other data sources.

Hundreds of pre-made spreadsheets and models are eligible for free. These will help you save time or give you ideas for creating your own worksheets.

Excel is, without a doubt, the most robust and adaptable technology ever created. Many careers and college students need basic awareness and familiarity with Excel, as well as Word and Outlook.

In the following sections, we'll show you how to use Excel in its most simple form. We'll go through the most popular toolbar (Ribbon) commands, as well as how to make a new spreadsheet and format it, save it, and print it. You'll also learn how to use 30 of the most commonly encountered formulas and functions, as well as a step-by-step example of how to build a simple Pivot Table.

When you're finished, you'll have a good understanding of Excel and be able to move forward to the next level of your Microsoft Office suite learning.

Chapter 1: Navigating excel

To begin, we'll first review how to open Excel and create a blank spreadsheet.

STARTING EXCEL

To open Excel:

1. Click the **'Start'** (Windows) button and scroll to the letter **'E.'**

2. Select the program **'Excel'**

This method is for Excel **version 2019**; earlier versions would be accessed differently.

Alternatively:

From the taskbar, select the Excel icon:

CREATING A NEW SPREADSHEET (STEP-BY-STEP EXAMPLE)

Once Excel has opened, your screen will look similar to the following:

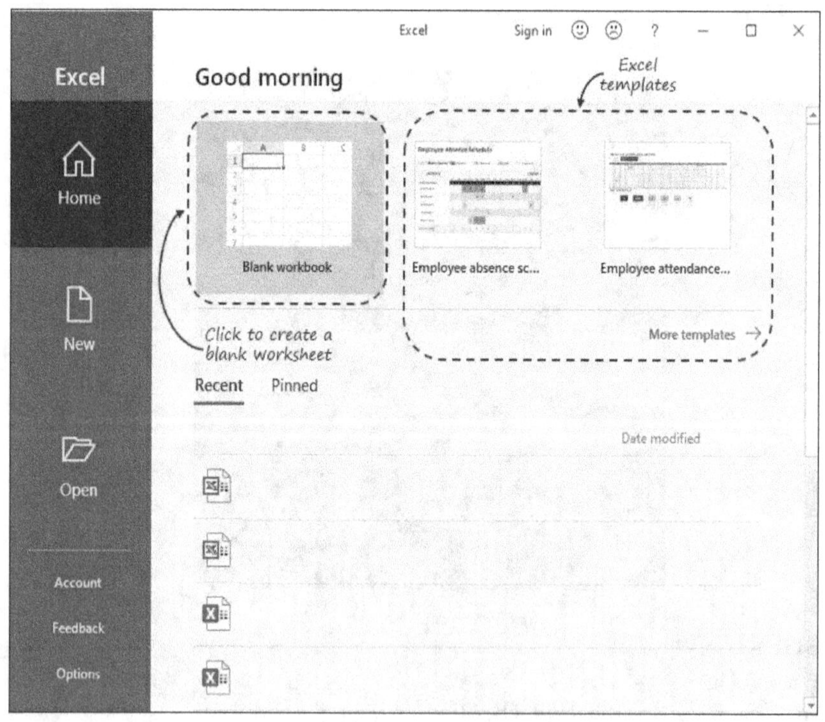

You'll notice pre-made templates available. The best practice is to first learn the basic functionality of Excel before using these. Once you have a better understanding of Excel, you may modify and verify the calculations in these templates meet your requirements.

1. Select the **'Blank Workbook'** option

After you click the **'Blank Workbook'** option, you will have created a **'workbook'** file made up of one or more worksheets.

The entire screen is not displayed for easier viewing:

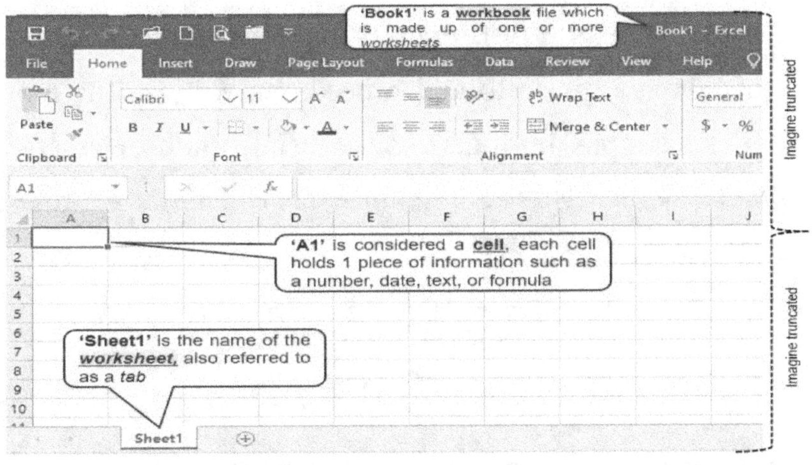

Next, let's review how to navigate and customize the toolbar (Ribbon) and Quick Access Toolbar.

TOOLBAR (RIBBON)

The **toolbar,** or what Microsoft calls the **'Ribbon,'** consists of tabs that contain commands. There are ten default tabs.

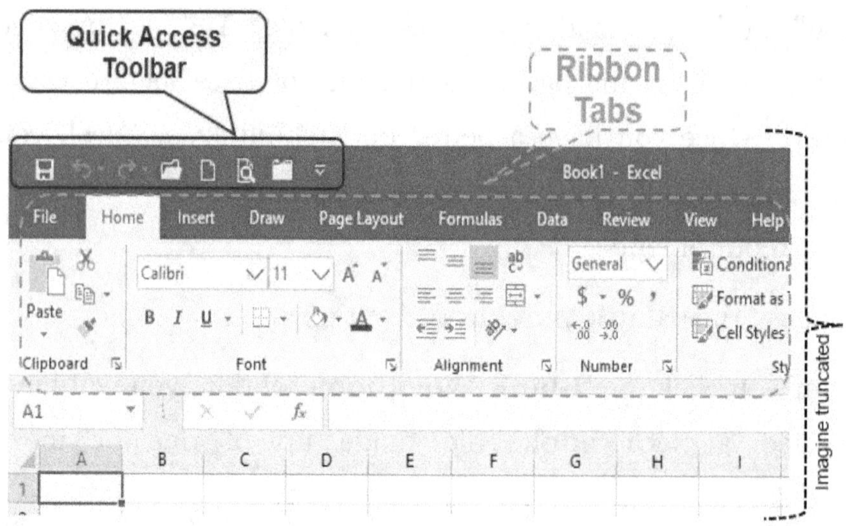

QUICK ACCESS TOOLBAR

The **Quick Access Toolbar** sets on top of the **Ribbon.** Think of this as a place to add procedures you use the most often. For example, buttons to save, print, undo or create a new workbook file. These commands stay constant, regardless of what Ribbon tab is active.

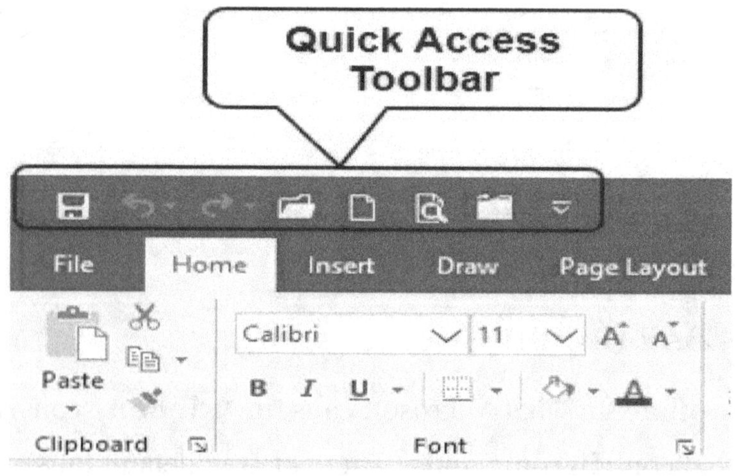

CUSTOMIZING THE RIBBON & QUICK ACCESS TOOLBAR

Both the **Quick Access Toolbar** and the **Ribbon** are customizable. I find it more efficient to modify the Quick Access Toolbar. However, you may prefer to change the Ribbon.

Below are the steps to remove or add buttons to both the Quick Access Toolbar and Ribbon.

To **add** a command button:

1. Click the drop-down arrow on the **'Quick Access Toolbar.'**

2. Select 'More Commands....'

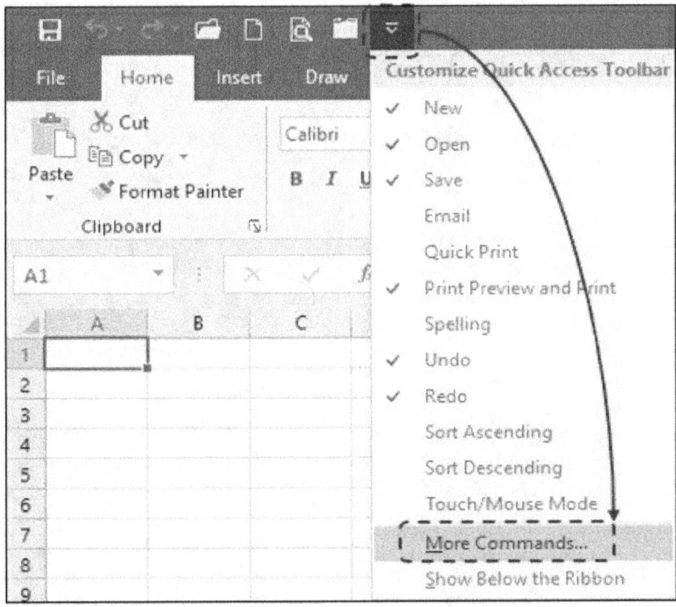

Alternatively, you may **right-click** over the **'Ribbon'** or the **'Quick Access Toolbar** to receive the below prompt:

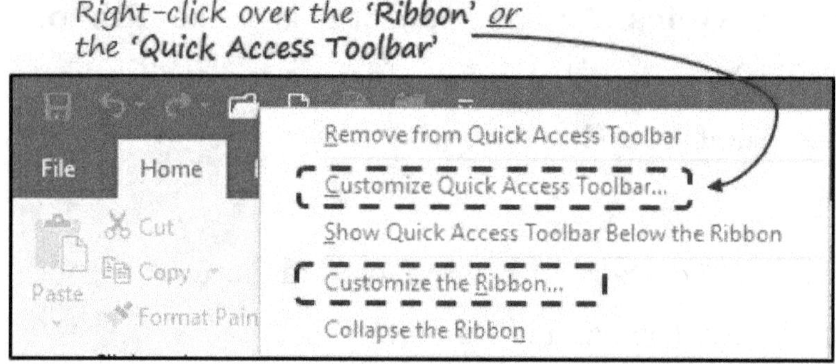

The following prompt will appear:

3. Select either **'Quick Access Toolbar'** or **'Customize Ribbon.'**

4. Select a command you would like to add

5. Select the **'Add>>'** button

6. Click the **'OK'** button

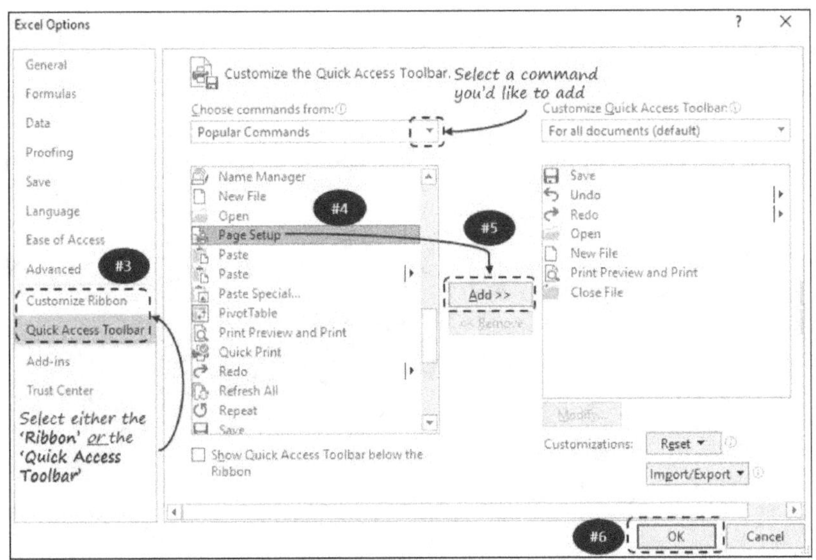

To **remove** a command button:

1. Click the drop-down arrow on the **'Quick Access Toolbar.'**

2. **Select 'More Commands...' 3. Select either 'Quick Access Toolbar' or 'Customize Ribbon.'**

3. Select a command you would like to remove

4. Select the **'<<Remove'** button

5. Click the **'OK'** button

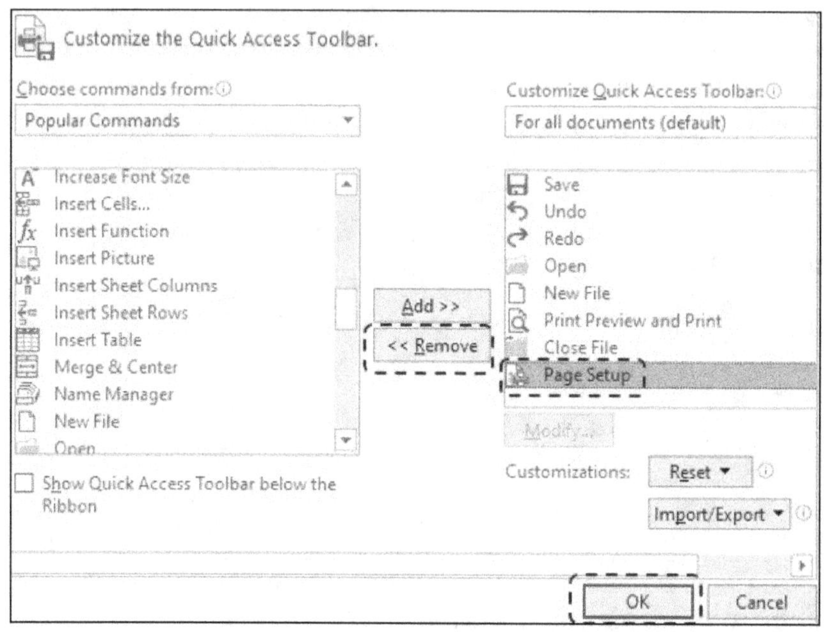

RIBBON & WORKBOOK DISPLAY OPTIONS

Across from the Quick Access Toolbar in the top left corner, you'll notice a series of small icons.

The up-arrow button, when clicked, will present three Ribbon choices:

- **Auto-hide Ribbon** covers the Ribbon before you unhide it by clicking the top of a worksheet.

- **Show Tabs** displays the tab name only, but not the individual commands

- **Show Tabs and Commands** displays both the tab name and the commands (this is the default setting).

The underscore button, when clicked, will **minimize** the active workbook

The double window button, when clicked, will **resize** the active workbook

The cross (X) button, when clicked, will **close** the active workbook (you'll be prompted to save your file if you've not already done so)

Lastly, let's take a quick look at a few more parts of the worksheet before we delve into the specifics of the Ribbon menu options.

NAME BOX

The **'Name Box'** indicates the location of the active cell

FORMULA BAR

The **'Formula Bar'** displays the **'syntax'** of a formula or displays a number, date, currency, or text value of the active cell.

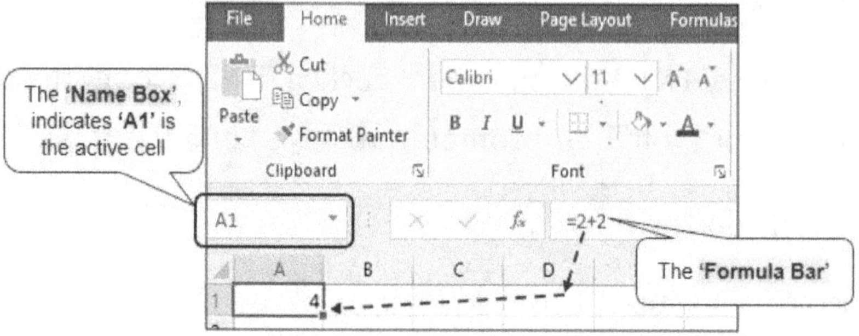

Syntax

> **Syntax** in Excel® refers to the arrangement or order of a formula or function. All formulas & functions begin with the equal sign (=) followed by numbers or the function's name.

Chapter 2: The Excel Ribbon Menu Descriptions

As we go through the Ribbon menus, you'll see that the same features can be accomplished in a variety of forms. You may, for example, print a worksheet by:

1. Choose a file from the Ribbon File: Clicking the 'Print' icon and printing

2. Extending the 'Page Setup' submenu and pressing the 'Print' icon from the Ribbon Page Layout

3. From the 'Quick Access Toolbar,' press the 'Print Preview and Print' key, then the 'Print' button.

4. Pressing shortcut keys **(CTRL + P)** on your keyboard and tapping the 'Print' icon

There is no superior method; it is merely a question of personal choice.

Following that, we'll go through eight of the ten Ribbon menus. The summary would include the key features of eight menus, although not all of the available commands will be covered. The usefulness of the 'Draw' and 'Page Layout' menus is not tested since it is covered in other parts of the book or is infrequently utilized.

File

The 'FILE' tab provides commands for saving, printing, and modifying the configuration of the Excel program.

FILES TO BE SAVED (STEP-BY STEP EXAMPLE)

To save a workbook file, follow these steps:

1. Click the 'Blank workbook' icon in the Excel program.

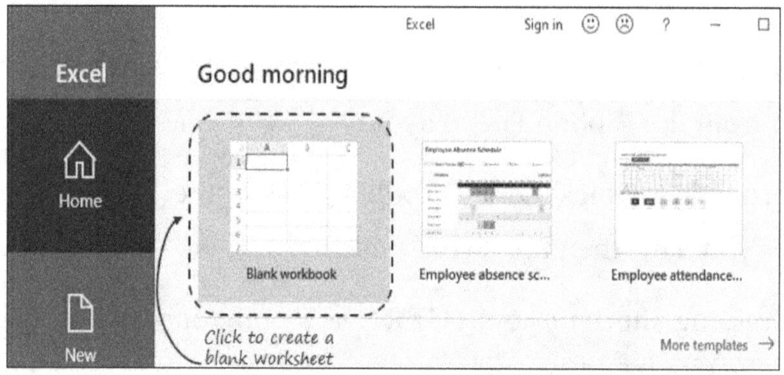

Enter the text **test** into cell **'A1'** 3. Click the **'File'** tab

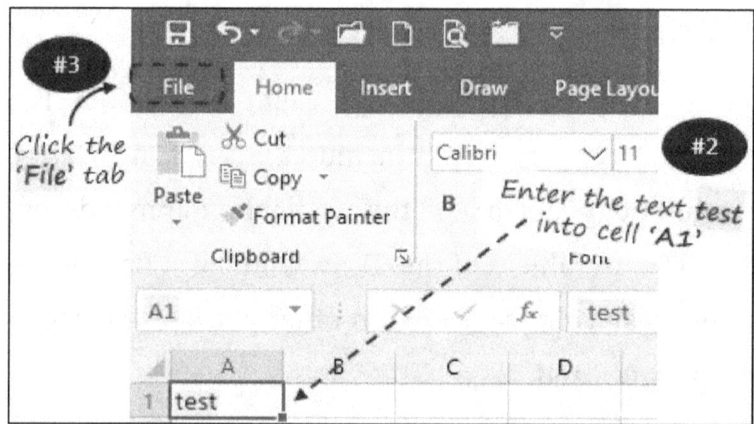

Click **'Save As'**

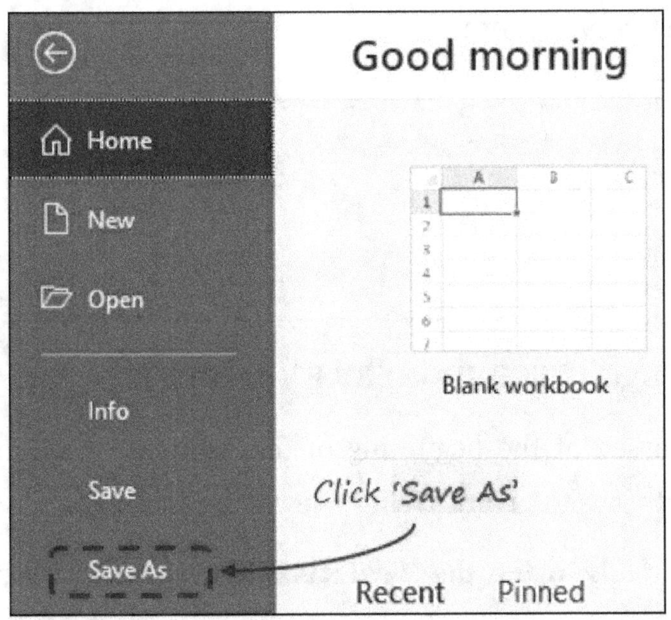

Click the **'Browse'** option to select a location on your computer to save the file

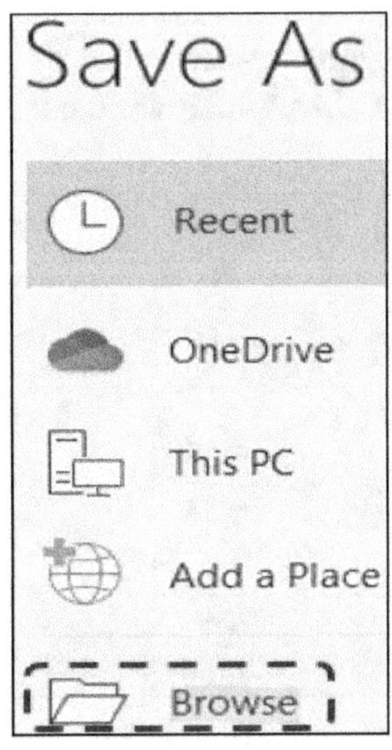

When prompted, provide the **File name: Test.xlsx**

Click the '**Save**' button

PRINTING (STEP-BY-STEP EXAMPLE)

As discussed at the beginning of this chapter, there are four different ways to print. We'll review three methods:

If not already, **open** the '**Test.xlsx**' file we created and saved in the previous section of this chapter:

1. Click the '**Open**' icon from the '**Quick Access Toolbar**' Click the '**Test.xlsx**' file to open

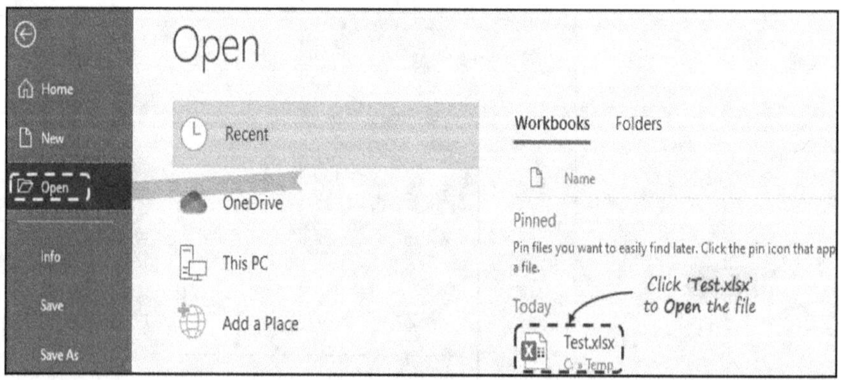

2. Click the '**File**' tab

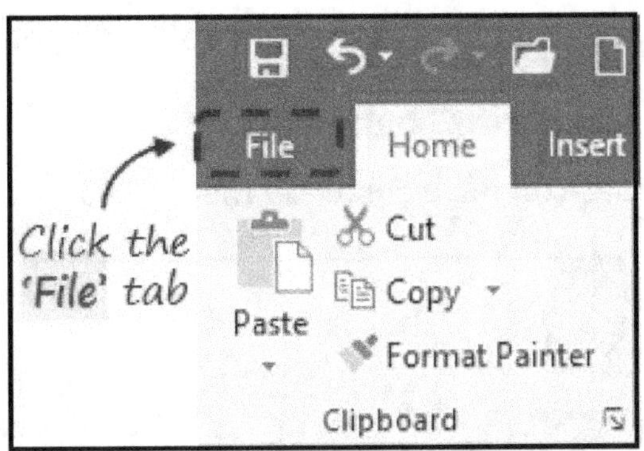

3. Click **'Print'**

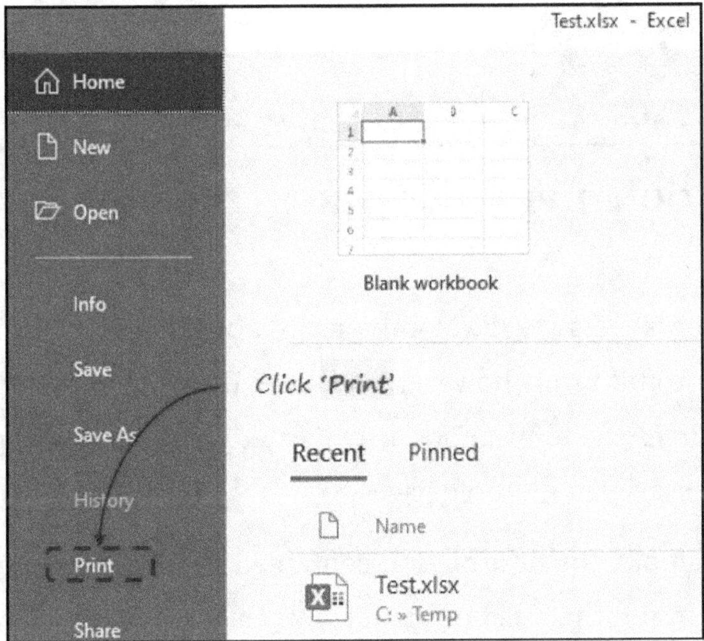

Alternatively:

Click the **'Print Preview and Print'** icon from the **'Quick Access Toolbar,'** once added to your 'Quick Access Toolbar.'

Using either approach will launch the following prompt

4. Click the **'Print'** button (the workbook would print assuming you have correctly installed a printer)

ADDITIONAL PRINT SETTINGS (THE PAGE LAYOUT TAB)

The worksheets we develop typically appear nicely formatted in electronic form; however, if a user prints the spreadsheet often times the information is truncated, and the report prints unnecessarily in multiple pages.

For example, the information contained in the below report is cut off in multiple sections and prints out in 3 pages. A reader would have a difficult time understanding the content or would be inconvenienced by having to adjust the print settings themselves.

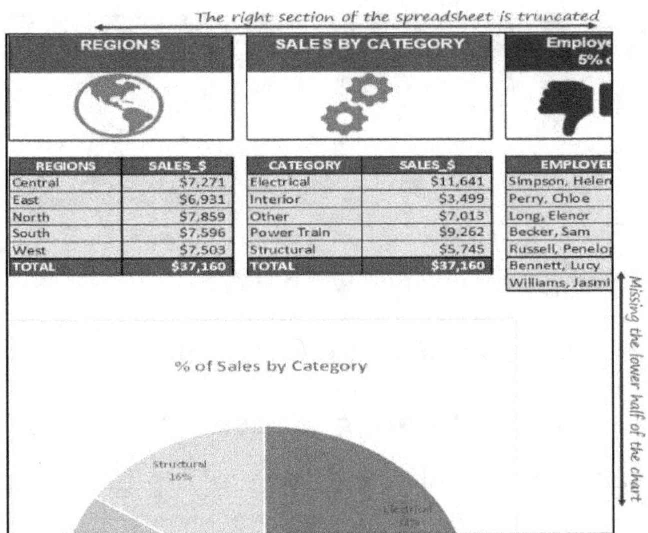

The following **is not** a step-by-step example, instead demonstrates through screenshots how to:

- Change the **'Orientation'** from **'Portrait'** to **'Landscape'**

- Adjust the margin settings

- Add a **Header or Footer** (page numbers)

The presentation uses the **Page Layout** menu from the Ribbon:

1. Expand the **'Page Setup'** section by clicking the diagonal arrow

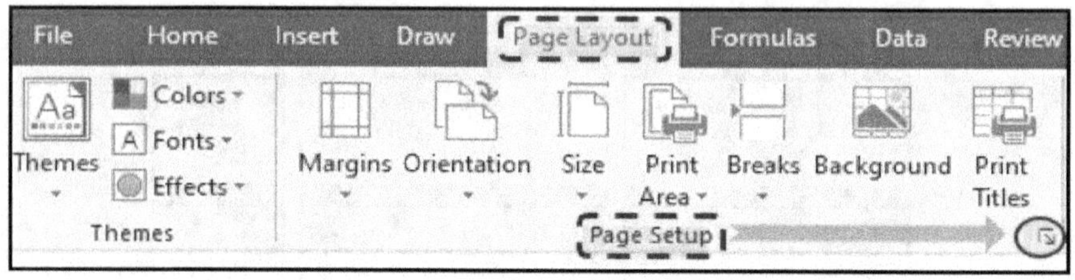

The following dialogue box will appear:

2. Select the **'Landscape'** radio button

3. Change the **'Scaling'** by selecting the **'Fit to'** radio button (this will ensure the report prints on 1 page)

4. Select the **'Margins'** tab

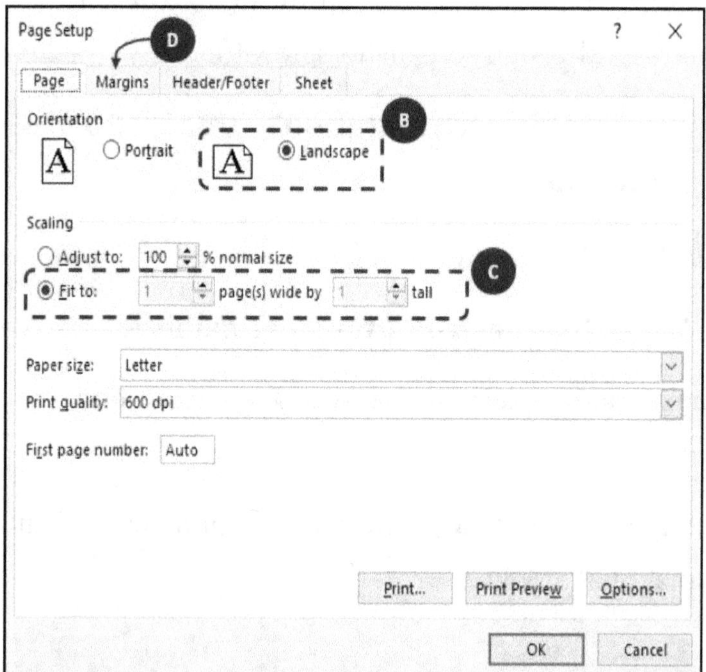

5. **Select the** 'Centre on page: Horizontally' **check box**

6. Select the **'Header/Footer'** tab

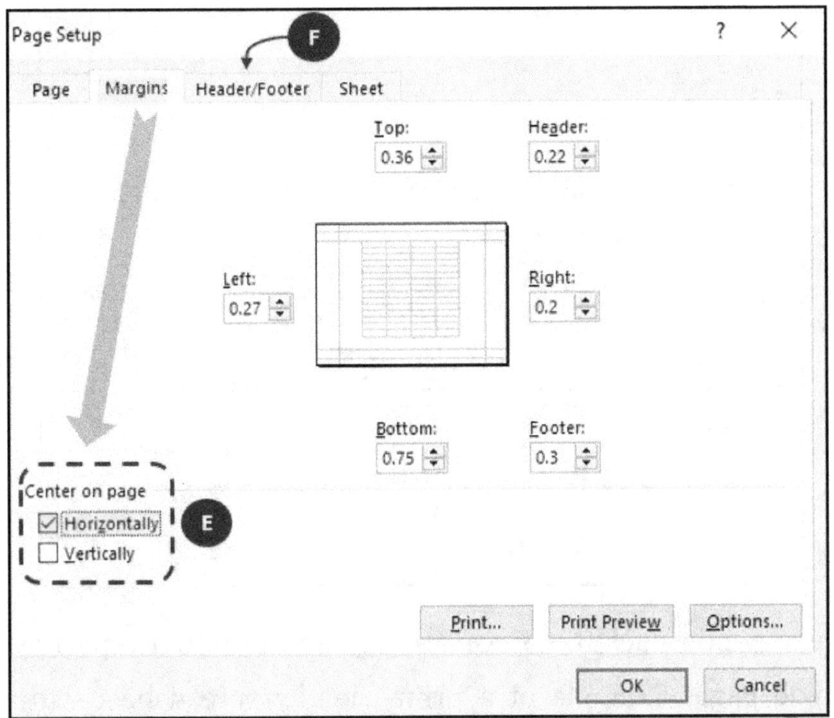

7. Select the button **'Custom Header...'** the title **'Monthly Dashboard'** was added

8. Select a drop-down list for **'Footer:'** by selecting **'Page 1 of?'**. The **'?'** will automatically populate to the number of pages selected for printing, i.e., Page 1 of **3**

9. Click the **'Print Preview'** button

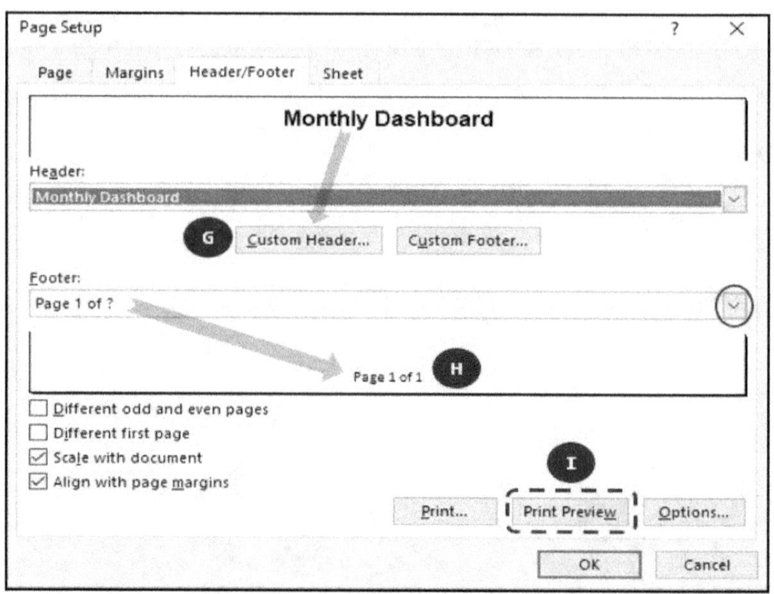

We may now click the **'Print'** button and print our report as a single page. Example of a print-friendly spreadsheet with a **Header & Footer** added:

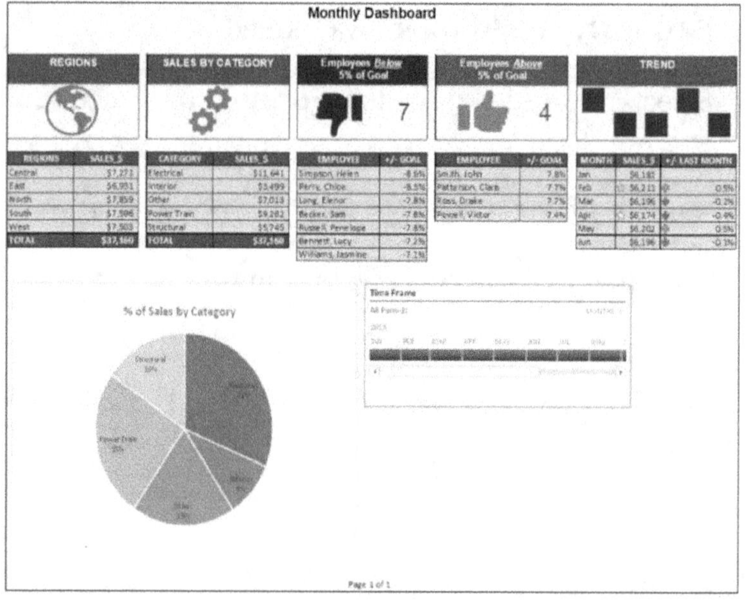

HOME

The **'Home'** tab is primarily used for formatting, which is changing the appearance of cell contents to improve readability or to draw focus to specific areas. Some of the most often used commands are:

- Copy, Cut, & Paste

- Font, Number, & Currency formatting

- Conditional Formatting

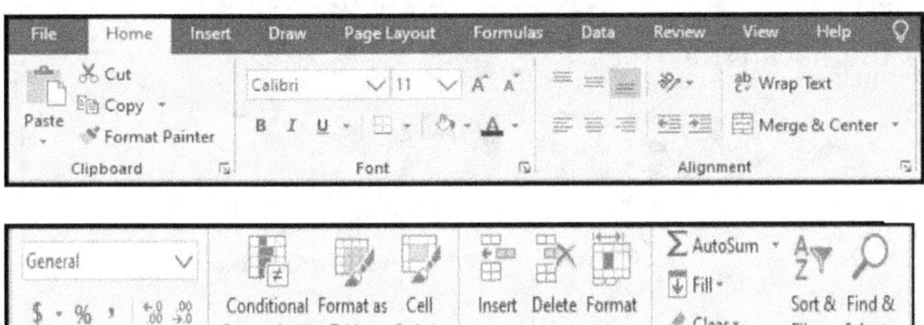

COPY

To **copy** the subjects of one more cell:

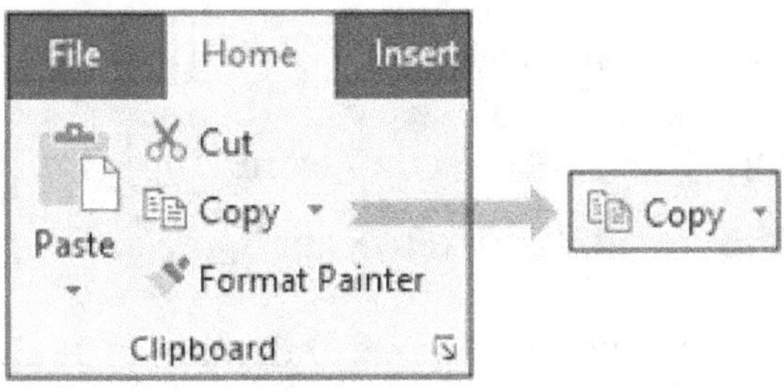

Select the cells you wish to copy and choose one of the following options:

From the **Ribbon: Home** (tab), click the **'Copy'** button (please see above screenshot)

Clicking the **'Copy'** icon from the **'Quick Access Toolbar'** - once added to your 'Quick **Access Toolbar.'**

Right-clicking over the cell(s) to be copied and select **'Copy.'**

CUT

To **cut**, remove the subjects of one more cell and move it to another location:

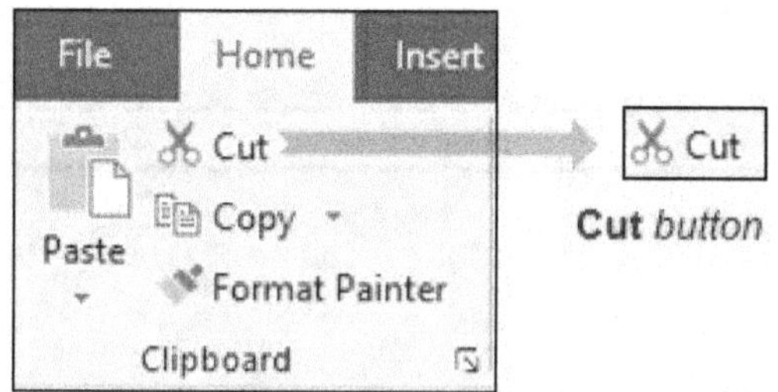

Select the cells you wish to cut (move) and choose one of the following options:

From the **Ribbon: Home** (tab), click the **'Cut'** button (please see above screenshot)

- Clicking the **'Cut'** icon from the **'Quick Access Toolbar'** - once added to your 'Quick Access Toolbar.'

- From your keyboard, press shortcut keys (**CTRL+X**)

- Right-clicking over the cell(s) to be cut and selecting '**Cut.**'

PASTE

To **paste** the subjects of one more cell <u>after</u> they have been copied or cut to another location:

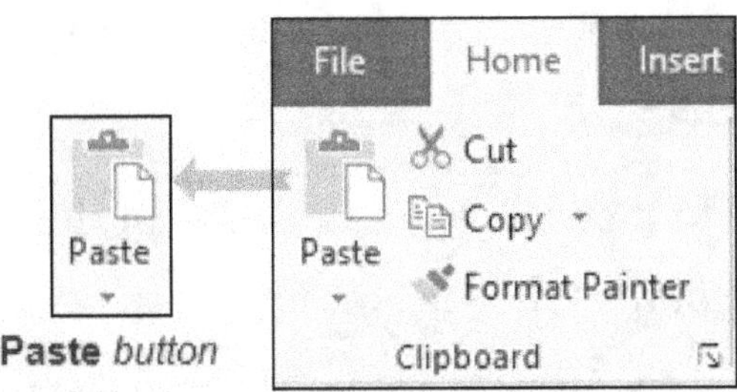

Paste *button*

Select the cells you wish to paste (move) and choose one of the following options:

From the **Ribbon: Home** (tab), click the '**Paste**' button (please see above screenshot)

Clicking the '**Paste**' icon from the '**Quick Access Toolbar**' - once added to your 'Quick Access Toolbar.'

From your keyboard, press shortcut keys (**CTRL+V**)

Clicking the '**Paste**' **drop-down arrow** and selecting one of the '**Paste Special**' commands:

The main '**Paste Special**' options are:

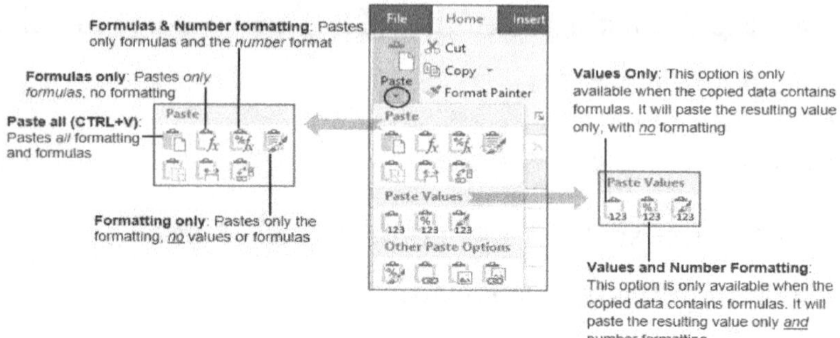

FONT OPTIONS

To change the font style, colour, and size of the subjects of the cell, select one of the following options:

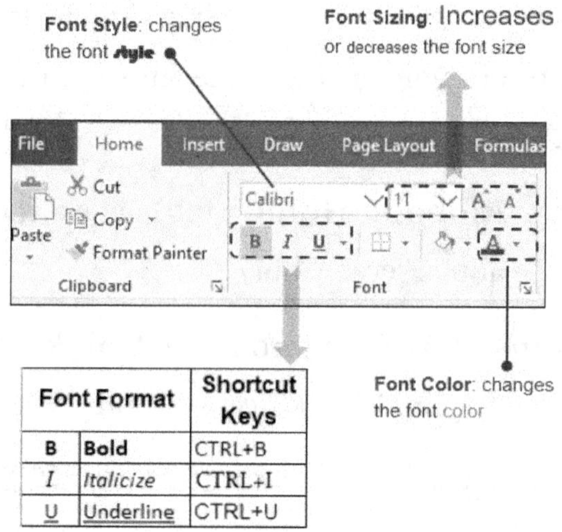

Font Format		Shortcut Keys
B	Bold	CTRL+B
I	Italicize	CTRL+I
U	Underline	CTRL+U

To add cell shading and/or gridlines:

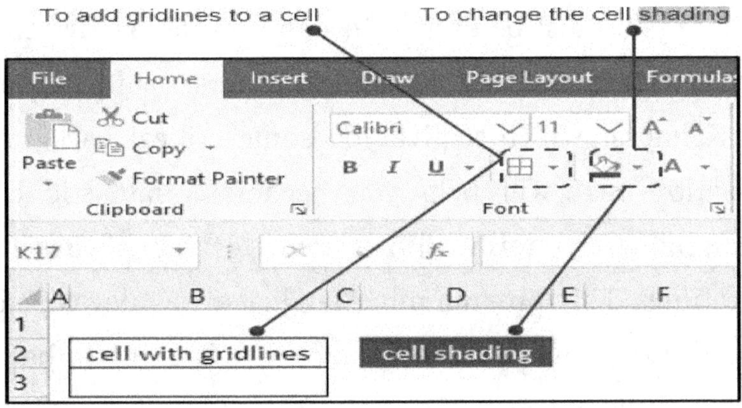

Chapter 3: Excel VBA

I am sure you must be excited to jump on the bandwagon of the Excel Programmers. Well, hold your horses a little for now, as this chapter will first give you some critical background information that will help you become a fantastic Excel Programmer. The term VBA stands for Visual Basic for Applications. This programming language was developed by Microsoft Company. VBA is the tool that is going to help us control and customize the functionalities of Excel.

Throughout this book, you will get to see the term "Macros" a lot as well. Before you confuse yourself, let me explain what macros is. The codes that are written to perform operations in excel is known as Macros. VBA, however, is the programming language platform where

Macros are written. This is how VBA and Macros are interlinked. The VBA tool can be convenient to perform thousands of different tasks. Here are a few scenarios:

- It can help in analysing data

- It can help us in forecasting and budgeting data

- Automating our reports to save up time and improve efficiency

- Conveying data into visuals such as charts, graphs, etc., the Word doc should look like the PDF file.

I can go on and on with the tasks it can perform, but hopefully, you do now have an idea about its functionalities. In a nutshell, the VBA tool helps to speed up the operations performed on excel. Let's take an example, every day; you get an excel sheet containing a list of employees with some necessary information. You have to manually perform some formatting like making the name bold, make the phone number right-aligned, and add some colours to the rows. Now, if the list of employees is long so doing it manually every day can be an extremely tedious task. This is basically where the VBA tool comes in handy. You can write a macro code regarding all the formatting steps, place a button on your sheet and finally bind the macros with the button. Just one hit, and you're good to go.

Jumping into the VBA Tool

Before we jump deep into the swimming pool, learning to swim should be our topmost agenda. This section is going to give you a feel of the entire VBA tool. It will give you a good grab on the basics.

To get started on the VBA tool, we first need to access the most crucial tab: Developer. Follow the steps to access the tab:

1. Open the Excel tool

2. Right Click on any area of the Ribbon and then select the customize option

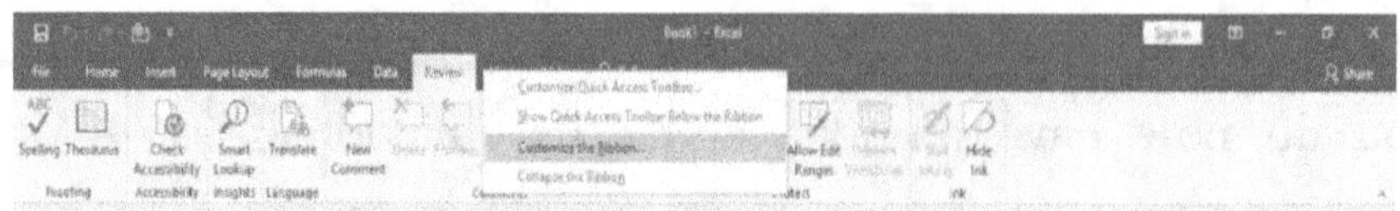

3. Once the customize tab is open, you can find the developer option in the second column

4. Check the Developer Option

5. Click Ok

Congratulations! You now have a brand-new tab on your Excel tool: Developer. By clicking on the developer tab, we will be navigated to the section that is of interest to all the VBA programmers.

We will now be performing our very first exercise on the VBA tool. The macro that we are going to write will perform the following functions:

- Type name into a cell

- Enter the current date and time into a cell

- Bold the text entered in the name cell

- Change the font size of the date cell to 14

Recording the Macros

In this section, we will be performing an exercise to learn how to record the Macros. Excel has a built-in functionality in which the user doesn't have to manually write the code. The tool has the option to record all the operations that you are performing and then finally generate a macro code for it. The macro we will write now won't win us the first prize in a VBA programming competition, but to reach your final destination, one needs to take baby steps. Following are the steps that we will follow to write our very first code.

1. Open the Excel Tool

2. Click on the developer tab

3. Select a cell on the excel worksheet. Click on any cell

4. On the developers' tab, click on the Record Macro Button

5. As shown below, the Record Macros box is displayed

6. Now we will be entering a name for the Macros. The default name is Macro 1, but its always advisable to give a better name.

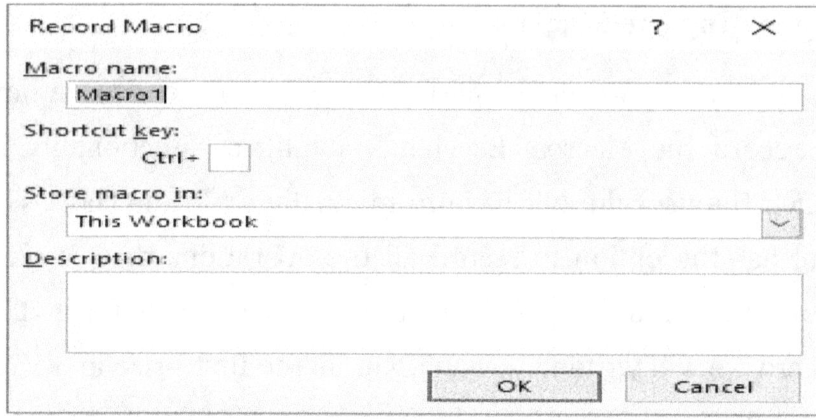

1. Click in the shortcut key and enter a shortcut key. For now, we will be entering shift+N, so our shortcut key will be ctrl+shift+N

2. On the macro dialogue box, the option that says "store in:" should be set to "This Workbook."

3. Click Ok. The macros will now start to record.

4. Type your name on the cell where you want to display it

5. Now in the adjacent cell, enter the below formula

6. Now we will convert the formula to its value. For this, right-click on the date cell, select copy. Now right-click on the cell again, and select paste values(V).

7. Now Select the cell where you entered your name. Go to the home tab, traverse to the font section and select bold(B). Also, change the font size to 14.

8. Now to stop recording, go to the developer section. Select stop recording.

Cheers! Your first project for the Excel VBA macro is finished.

To ensure that your macros are working fine, you should test your code. Move the cursor to an empty cell, press

Ctrl+Shift+N. Within a snap, the excel code will be executed. Your name, date, and time will be displayed on the sheet. You can also view the code that has been recorded by the excel tool. Go to the Developer tab, and click on macros. You can now view the code that was automatically generated.

Behind the operations that you just performed.

Below is the code that was generated.

```
Sub MyName()
'
' MyName Macro
'


    Range("B2").Select
    ActiveCell.FormulaR1C1 = "Anum"
    Range("C2").Select
    ActiveCell.FormulaR1C1 = "=NOW()"
    Range("B2").Select
    Selection.Font.Bold = True
    With Selection.Font
        .Name = "Calibri"
        .Size = 14
        .Strikethrough = False
        .Superscript = False
        .Subscript = False
        .OutlineFont = False
        .Shadow = False
        .Underline = xlUnderlineStyleNone
        .ThemeColor = xlThemeColorLight1
        .TintAndShade = 0
        .ThemeFont = xlThemeFontMinor
    End With
End Sub
```

The first statement recognizes the sub procedure and gives the name of the macro that you entered. The second statement identifies that cell "B2" is selected. B2 means a second column and second row on the excel sheet. The third statement then highlights the name you entered on Cell B2. Cell b3 is then selected, and then the Now () formula was entered. Selection. Font. bold= true indicates that the cell formatting was changed to bold. The sub-procedure finally ends the code by the End sub Procedure.

Let me introduce you to a real programming language element called a variable. Just like other programming languages, VBA has elements common to them. The main agenda of the VBA tool is to manipulate data. VBA can store

the data in the computer's memory. Some of the data that you create is stored in variables. A named storage location in the computer's memory is known as a variable. Excel gives us the flexibility to name the variables whatever we want them to be. To assign a value to the variable, we use the equal sign operator. Let's look at some of the examples of the variables.

```
a = 1
PerformanceRate = 0.95
EmployeeSalary = 123455
DataEntered = False
a = a + 1
UserName = "Anum Haroon"
```

There are specific rules when declaring variables in the VBA tool:

- The first letter of the variable should be a character.

- The rest can be numbers, letters, or punctuation characters

- There is no distinguishment between the upper-case and lower-case letters when declaring variables

- A variable name should be without any space

- Special characters such #, $, %, &, or! cannot be used in the variable name

- The size of the variable name should not exceed 255 characters

To better understand the variables, most programmers use mixed cases, for example, Performance Rate or Employee Salary.

The VBA tool also puts some restrictions on the variable names. Words such as Dim, End, With, Sub, Next, and for cannot be used by the programmers as these words are reserved by VBA. If any of these words arise in your code, you will get a compile error.

Getting Familiarize with the VBA Data Types

When I say the word data type, I am mainly referring to a way in which the program written in VBA stores data in memory.

VBA gives us the leverage not to assign a data type to every variable, but if you leave it on VBA, there's definitely some cost to it. The automatic assignment of data types may result in slower execution and wastage of memory.

Applications that are small in size may not be affected by the automatic declaration, but the large and complex application does have an impact on them. It's always a good

practice to declare the data type of the variables that you are going to use. Although the list is long, below are the most common types of data that VBA can handle.

Data type	Bytes Used	Range of Values
Byte	1	0 to 255
Boolean	2	True or False
Integer	2	-32768 to 32768
Long	4	-2,147,483,648 to 2,147,483,648
Double	8	-1.79E308 to -4.94E324 for negative values

Currency	8	-922,337,203,685,477 to 922,337,203,685,477
Date	8	1/1/0100 to 12/31/9999
String	1per chart	Varies
Variant	Varies	Varies

A good rule of thumb is to use the variable with the smallest size, but it should also serve your purpose.

Declaring Variables and their scope

By now, I am sure you must be familiarized with variables and their data types. In this section, we will now be declaring a variable to a data type. If a variable is not declared in your macros, the VBA itself will define it to default data type: Variant. For example, if a particular variable is by default set to be a variant and it contains a text string that looks like a number (e.g., 123), this variable, however, can be used for both the numeric and string calculations. As mentioned earlier, it is always a good practice to declare the data type of your variable. Else the VBA tool will assign the data type as a variant, and the

variant results in time-consuming checks, and this ultimately uses memory. One good way to force yourself to declare the data types of the variables is to write the following statement as the first statement in your VBA module:

```
Option Explicit
```

This statement forces you to declare all data types of your variables, as it will throw a compile error if any variable is left undeclared. A variable is using declared by using the Dim statement.

Let's look at some examples:

All the variables in the above example have been defined as a particular data type apart from the variable "X." The variable X will, however, be treated as a variable.

Apart from Dim, to declare variables, we can use three other keywords:

- Private

- Static

- Public

Let's look at an example to get a good picture of the declarations of the data type of variables.

```
Sub Variables()
Dim Name As String
Name = "Anum Haroon"

Dim Age As Integer
Age = 21

Dim Birthdate As Date
Birthdate = 19 / 11 / 1991

MsgBox "Name is " & Name & Chr(10) & "Age is " & Age & " And Birthdate is " & Birthdate

End Sub
```

When the above VBA code is executed, a message is prompted on the screen. The message box is as follows:

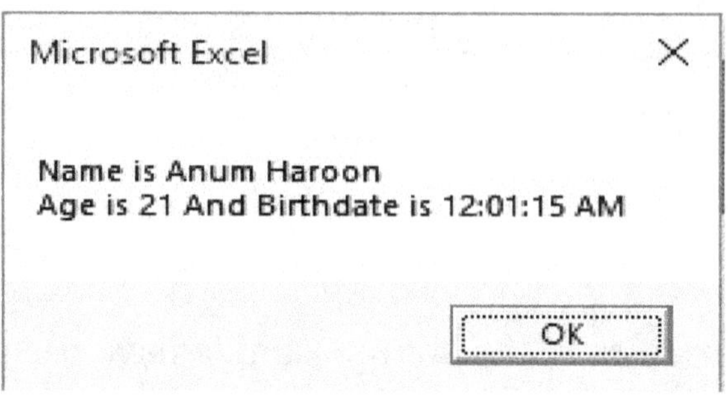

Strings Playing with characters

Now let's have fun by playing with the strings in the VBA tool. Strings fundamentally compromise characters that are arranged in a sequence. The characters in the string can consist of alphabets, special characters, numbers, or any of these. The characters in the string must be enclosed with double-quotes.

There are numerous functionalities of the string. The table below displays some of the functions that are performed on strings.

Function name	Returns
Str ()	A string representation of a number

Val ()	A numerical representation of a number
Trim ()	To remove spaces in a string
Left ()	To get a portion of the string from the left side
Right ()	To extract a portion from the right side
Mid ()	To extract any part of the string
Len ()	To retrieve the number of characters in the string

StrCov ()	To convert the string to some another format
UCase ()	Convert all characters to uppercase
LCase ()	Convert all characters to lower case

The Excel VBA handles two types of strings:

- Fixed-Length Strings

- Variable-Length Strings

As far as the fixed-length strings are concerned, they mainly contain a fixed number of characters. The maximum number of characters they can store is 65,526. The second type of string is the Variable-Length String. The variable-length string can store a massive number of characters. Whenever you declare a string, it's always a good practice to declare the maximum length of the string; otherwise, the VBA tool will handle it on its own. Below is an example of declaring a fixed-length string.

```
Dim MyName As String * 20
```

Let's write a macro code and play with some functionalities of the string. I would like to call the procedure "Play_With_Strings."

```
Sub Play_With_Strings()

Dim Name As String
Dim FirstName As String
Dim LastName As String
Dim SpaceLoc As Integer

Name = "Anum Haroon"

SpaceLoc = InStr(1, Name, " ")

FirstName = Left(Name, SpaceLoc - 1)

LastName = Mid(Name, SpaceLoc + 1, Len(Name) - SpaceLoc)

MsgBox (" The full name is " & Name & ", the first name

is " & FirstName & " and the last name is " & LastName)

End Sub
```

Now let's decode it step-by-step. The first four statements in the procedure are the part where the variables are declared. All the first three variables have been set as strings, and the last one has been declared as an integer. Now, after the variable declaration section, we begin by assigning values to the variables. I first stored a name in the Name variable. Now next, I wanted to find out the location of the space between my first name and the last name. Space is located through the InStr () function. The InStr () has three input parameters. The first parameters decide from where position the function should start searching in the string. The second parameter is the string that needs to be traversed, and finally, the third parameter defines what needs to be searched. In this example, in the variable value "Anum Haroon," we want to search the location of the space. Once this is found out, the value is stored in the SpaceLoc variable. Now we want to retrieve the first and last names and then store them in the variables, respectively. To do this, we will be using the Left () and Mid () functions of the string. The Left () function has two inputs. The first input is the string, whereas the second input defines the position where the string needs to be extracted. So, by passing the SpaceLoc and the Name variable, we can get the first name. To get the last name, we will be using the Mid () function. The Mid () Function has three inputs that are the string, the start, and the end position. We will be passing the name variable, the SpaceLoc position, and then the end position, which is basically equal to the string length. The last statement is written in the VBA Code to generate an output on the screen. We will again be binding the VBA code to a button. Once the button is executed, the following values will pop up on the screen.

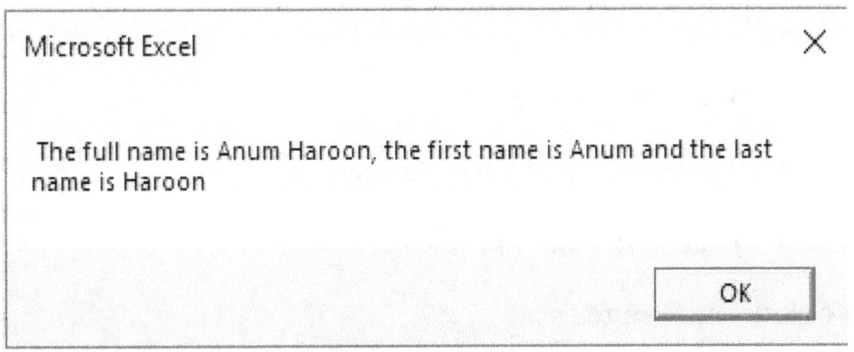

Not too bad prospective Programmers! You now must be having a good understanding of how you can play with the string functions. String function can be convenient, especially when you have to manipulate large datasets. Instead of retrieving all the functionality manually, you can write a macro code, bind it with a button, and you're good to go.

VBA Macros Jumping to an advanced level So far, we have covered some basics of the VBA Macros. We will now be pacing up our game by jumping over to an advanced level.

VBA Macros has considerably made the lives of excel users easy. With the implementation of VBA Macros in your worksheet, you can significantly save up time by automating your operations of excel. Instead of working on large data sets manually, formatting thousands of records, applying formulas to manipulate data, you can write a VBA Macro, bind it with the excel sheet and do all the operations within seconds.

In this section, we will be working on some examples of VBA Macros. This section will compromise of the following subtopics:

- Worksheet Ranges

- Exploring some Excel Settings

- Pacing up your VBA Code

Worksheet Ranges

The VBA programming has got a lot to do with the ranges on the worksheet. The following points need to be kept in mind whenever we are working with range objects:

- If you are not associating the worksheet name to the range in your code, then you must ensure that the sheet on which you want your macros to run must be in the active state

- Excel gives the users the ability to select multiple ranges

- The Macro recorder doesn't always create the best code. You can always edit the Macro generated code to make it more efficient

One of the most frequently used operations of the Excel Macros is copying a range. If you are using the macro recorder to generate a code while copying a range, you will get the below code.

```
Sub Range()

    Range("A1:A5").Select

    Selection.Copy

    Range("B1").Select

    ActiveSheet.Paste

    Application.CutCopyMode = False

End Sub
```

One other operation of the range function is the Selection ability. We often want to select a block of cells and then do some operations on it. Instead of giving reference to each cell, we can collectively refer to the entire block of cells in one statement. Please find below an example of the Selection operation on the range statement.

```
Sub Select_Range_Down()

   Range(ActiveCell, ActiveCell.End(xlDown)).Select

End Sub
```

In the above code, the VBA procedure is beginning to select the cells from the active cell. It is then extending the range until a blank cell

arises.

```
Sub Select_Range_Down()

  Range(ActiveCell, ActiveCell.End(xlDown)).Select

End Sub
```

One other exciting feature of VBA Macros is the selection of the entire column or the entire row. The following is an example of the selection of the entire row.

```
    Sub SelectRow()

      ActiveCell.EntireRow.Select

    End Sub
```

Similarly, the entire column functionality of excel can also be used to select the entire column.

Exploring some Excel Settings

The operation of some procedures in Excel Macros can be changed by one or more Excel settings. One interesting setting is the Boolean setting. In this setting, you give a False or a True value to the excel procedure, and then the setting is altered accordingly. Let's look at an example. In Excel

Macros, you can give page breaks on your worksheet. You can turn on the Page break feature of excel by passing a real value to the DisplayPageBreaks procedure.

```
ActiveSheet.DisplayPageBreaks = True
```

Similarly, we can turn off this feature by passing a false value.

```
ActiveSheet.DisplayPageBreaks = False
```

Pacing up your VBA Code

VBA is the first way to perform data manipulations on your worksheet. In this section, we will be discussing some useful tips to further optimize the VBA Code to pace your operations.

One feature of excel is that whenever you execute the Excel Macros, the updates are visible on the screen. This, however, can have an impact on the performance of your code. You can, however, disable the setting. To do this, write down the below code.

```
Application.ScreenUpdating = False
```

This will turn off the screen updates while the Macros is being executed. To turn on the feature again, execute the below code.

```
Application.ScreenUpdating = True
```

One other way to speed up your Macros is by disabling the automatic calculation feature. If there are a lot of complicated formulas on your worksheet, setting the calculation mode to the manual can significantly speed up things in your code. Execute the below statement to make the calculation manual.

```
Application.Calculation = xlCalculationManual
```

Macros display alerts messages to the users while the code is being executed. In this case, if the Excel is unattended and the Macros is executing, then the alert message will bring the code to a halt. They require humans to respond to the alert messages. However, there is an option to disable the alert messages so that the Macros is not brought to a halt.

```
Application.DisplayAlerts = False
```

You can also turn the alerts by writing a statement at the end of your code. To do this, we will just change the Display Alerts statements to a True condition.

```
Application.DisplayAlerts = True
```

Another to pace up the speed of your Macro Program is to ensure that you declare variables at the start of your code. It is imperative that you declare the data type of all the variables. However, Excel doesn't throw an error if a variable's data type is left undefined, but Excel won't know the exact size of the variable. As a result of this, Excel might assign space much more extensive than what is required. This will result in extra memory consumption and can also decrease the performance of your code.

Loops Repeating blocks of VBA

Loops are essential as they make macros more capable, and they also make the code easier to write. Instead of writing numerous statements for every cell on the worksheet, loops help to simplify your code. Several types of loops are supported in VBA.

For-Next loop in the programming language is referred to as the simplest type of loop. There is a control variable that acts as a counter to the loop condition. The counter begins from the start value and continues to be executed till the end value is reached. Code that is written between the for statement and the next statement is repeated in the loop. Let's look at an example.

```
Sub Multiply()
  Dim Product As Double
  Dim Counter As Integer
  Product = 0
  For Counter = 1 To 50
  Product = Product * Counter
  Next Counter
  MsgBox Product
  End Sub
```

In the above example, we are performing a multiplication operation in the For-Next Loop. The counter will begin from 1 and continue to execute till the counter value is reached 50. There is the only statement written in the For-Next loop. The statement multiplies the counter value with the Product value and stores it in the Product variable. When the For-Next loop counter value is reached 50, the Product value will be displayed on the screen. However, it is not advisable to change the counter value in the For-Next Statement as it can generate unpredictable results. The for-Next loop can also include an Exit statement within the block. The Exit statements are placed in the For-Next block to terminate the loop immediately.

In the following example, an Exit Statement has been inserted in the For-Next loop.

```
Sub Exit_Statement()
    Dim a As Integer
    a = 10
    For i = 0 To a
        MsgBox ("The value is i is : " & i)
        If i = 4 Then
            i = i * 10
            MsgBox ("The value is i is : " & i)
            Exit For
        End If
    Next
End Sub
```

The MsgBox will display the value of i. The value of i is incremented. As shown in the above example, when the value of I will be equal to 4, the code will enter in the if statement. In the if statement, the value of i is first multiplied by 10, and then it will be printed on the screen. Soon after this, an exit statement will be executed, which will end the loop immediately. When the above code is executed, the following output will be displayed on the screen sequentially.

```
The value is i is : 0

The value is i is : 1

The value is i is : 2

The value is i is : 3

The value is i is : 40
```

The exit statements can be beneficial, especially when we want to handle exceptions or errors in our code. If, for example, there is a chance that a garbage value can come in a specific variable. I don't handle the garbage value; there is a chance that the loop will be executed till infinity. This can result in memory overload. To cater to this scenario, the exit statements are placed so that the loop is terminated immediately.

Another type of loop is the Nested For-Next loop. The nested statement comes in handy when you want to loop through tabular data or multidimensional data. A table has data placed in both columns and rows. One loop is used to traverse through the columns, whereas the other loop can be used to traverse through the rows. This is how you use the nested For-Next loop. In the following example, we will be filling up data in both the rows and the columns.

```vba
Sub Fill_Table()
Dim Col As Long
Dim Row As Long
Dim i As Integer
i = 0
For Col = 1 To 3
For Row = 1 To 3
i = i + 1
Cells(Row, Col) = i
Next Row
Next Col
End Sub
```

In this example, we will be filling up a 3 columns x 3 rows table. The outer for loop fills up the data in the columns, whereas the inner for loop fills up the data in the rows. The output of the code can be seen below.

	A	B	C
1	1	4	7
2	2	5	8
3	3	6	9
4			

Another type of looping structure which is supported the VBA is the Do-While loop. The statements in the Do-While will keep on repeatedly executing until the mentioned condition is fulfilled.

```vba
Sub DoWhileDemo()

  Do While ActiveCell.Value <> Empty

  ActiveCell.Value = ActiveCell.Value * 2

  ActiveCell.Offset(1, 0).Select

  Loop

End Sub
```

In the above example, a Do-While loop is inserted. The Do statement checks whether the active cell is empty or not. If the cell is not empty, the active cell is multiplied by, and then the next cell is select. Whenever the code encounters an empty cell, the do-while loop will break. One should always ensure that there should be some break statement in the loop; else, the loop will keep on executing till infinity. This, however, can result in

memory overflow. Loops considerably save up the space of the code and make it look compact and less complicated. However, loop statements do not reduce the time the code takes to execute.

Arrays Storing collection of elements

Arrays are usually supported by all programming languages. Arrays are also supported by VBA, thus making life easier for programmers. An array is used where we want to collect data of a similar type into one single variable. In an array, data is stored in a sequential manner. Each element in the array is provided an index number. The index number can be stated as a reference to the elements stored in the array. For example, we can define an array to store the names of the days of the week. If the array is named as Weekdays, the first element in the array will be stated as Weekdays (1). Similarly, the second element will be stated as Weekdays (2), the third as Weekdays (3), and so on. In order to use the array, it is mandatory to first declare the data type of array. VBA does not give us the flexibility to leave an array undeclared. Just like other regular variables, an array can be declared by either using a Dim statement or a Public statement. However, one additional thing about the array is that you need to mention the number of elements the array will hold. The syntax for declaring an array can be seen below.

```
Dim Dec_Array(0 To 10) As Integer
```

You declare the first index number, the keyword To, and then finally the last index number. All this is enclosed inside the parentheses. One flexibility VBA offers is that you don't necessarily have to mention the lower index every time. In this case, VBA assumes that the lower index is 0. For example, the above statement can also be written as:

```
Dim Dec_Array(10) As Integer
```

VBA, by default, assumes the lower index to be zero. However, if you don't want VBA to assume the lower index to zero, you can use the Option Base statement to force VBA to change the lower index accordingly. For example, if you want VBA to assume the lower index to be always set to 1, then you should write:

```
Option Base 1
```

You also need to ensure that this statement is written before the declaration of the array.

So far, we have discussed one-dimensional arrays. A more natural explanation of the one-dimensional array is a single line of a value of the same data type. When we want to have more than one dimension in an array, this is known as the multi-dimensional array. VBA can handle up to 60 dimensions in a multi-dimensional array. However, this is a sporadic case in which 60 dimensions are being used in the VBA code. A multidimensional array is also declared using the Dim statement.

```
Dim Multi_Dim(1 To 10, 1 To 100) As String
```

This is a multi-dimensional array. The first index of the multidimensional array ranges from 1 to 10, whereas the range for the second index is from 1 to 100. This results in the declaration of 1000 elements in the array. The numbers are stored in a tabular arrangement of 10 rows x 100 columns. To refer to any element in the array, you have to mention two index numbers. The first index number will be the row, and the second index number will be the column. For example, if we want to assign a value to the element in the 2nd row and 4th column, we will write it as:

```
Multi_Dim(2, 4) = 10
```

The value 10 will be stored in the element of the array that is placed in the 2nd row and 4th column. Dynamic arrays are also supported by VBA. The advantage of using a dynamic array is that you don't have to declare the number of elements it will hold at the start of your code. The array size is declared at runtime. Dynamic arrays help to save memory.

Functions Performing Specific Tasks

Let's first define what exactly a function is. A function can be called a procedure that performs some sort of calculation. A function returns a single value. Let's take an example; the Sum function will return the sum of the values that it will intake. Similarly, in VBA macros, the function undergoes a specific calculation and then finally returns a single value.

The function that you utilize in your VBA code primarily comes from three areas:

- Worksheet functions

- Some Built-in functions

- Customize functions that are defined according to your needs

Playing with built-in functions

Well, the good thing about using VBA is that it has made the life of a programmer easy by defining some built-in Functions. You don't have to write every function from scratch. You just need to know the exact name of the function and Voila!

Let's look at some built-in functions of the VBA tool.

```
Sub DisplayDate()

MsgBox "The Date is: " & Date

End Sub
```

The above procedure has been created to display the system date. In this scenario, we have used the built-in excel function, Date. The Date function doesn't require any input arguments. We can also retrieve the time by writing Time instead of Date. Time again is also a built-in the function of the excel tool.

Let's look at another example:

```
Sub Get_String_Length()

Dim Name As String
Dim StringLength As Integer

Name = "Anum Haroon"
StringLength = Len(Name)

MsgBox Name & " has " & StringLength & " characters"


End Sub
```

In the above example, we wanted to retrieve the string length of the name. We, therefore, used the excel built-in function, Len ().

If we want to retrieve the year or the month from the system date.

```
Sub Display_Month()

Dim Month_Name As Long

Month_Name = Month(Date)

MsgBox MonthName(Month_Name)



End Sub
```

In the above procedure, we are basically using the Built-in Month function to retrieve the Month from the System Date. Further, we are also using the Month Name Function in order to display the month name.

There are specific functions in the VBA tool that come up with some additional functionalities. For example, the MsgBox is a convenient function. Every time a user uses the MsgBox function in its Macros, a screen is popped up at whatever line it is executed. This MsgBox can be very handy to prompt the user about the values that are stored in the variables. Moreover, it

also helps to debug the code and find out any potential errors in the code. There is another convenient function which is known as the Input Box function. The Input Box function gives the user the capability to enter a value into a simple box that is displayed. The value that is retrieved through the Input Box can be further manipulated in the macros that we have written.

The VBA tool facilitates the user with lots of built-in functionality. The question is that how do you locate those functions? Well, that's not an issue at all. You can retrieve a list of all the built-in function by typing VBA followed by a period as shown in the diagram below

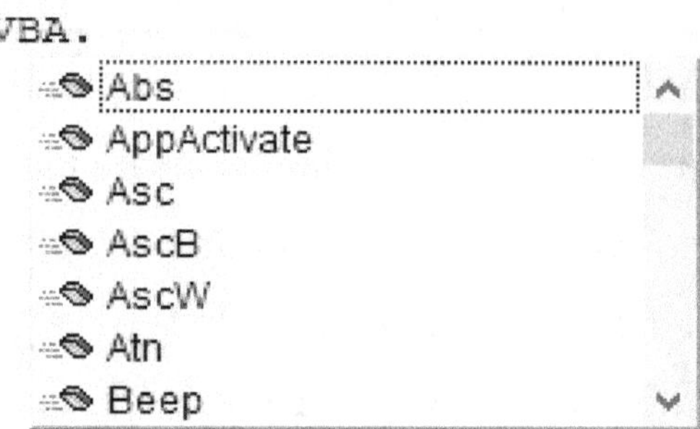

In order to find out the details linked to a particular function, enter the name of the function in the VBA module, move the pointer on the text and then press F1. You will be prompted with a new window screen, and the help wizard will open up.

Although the list of inbuilt functions is exceptionally long, I have compiled some important ones in the table below.

Exploring the worksheet functions

One other interesting feature of the Excel VBA is the worksheet functions. A worksheet is an area where the cells are placed, and the data is manipulated on the cells. In a nutshell, the worksheet is the workspace where basically all the calculations and the manipulations take place. When we are accessing functions using the "Worksheet Function" expression, the manipulation or calculation is performed on the active sheet. By active sheet, I basically mean the sheet that is currently open on the screen.

Let's look at an example of a worksheet's sum function.

```
Total_Amount = Application.WorksheetFunction.Sum(Range("B1:B3"))
```

In the above example, "Total Amount" is the variable in which the sum of the cells is being stored. Range ("B1: B3") refers to the cells on the worksheet of which the sum has to be taken. VBA also gives user's to access the Sum function directly either from the Application part of the Worksheet Function part. VBA has the ability to figure out what exactly you are performing. Smart Right? The following three statements have exactly the same output.

```
Total_Amount = Application.WorksheetFunction.Sum(Range("B1:B3"))

Total_Amount = WorksheetFunction.Sum(Range("B1:B3"))

Total_Amount = Application.Sum(Range("B1:B3"))
```

I personally prefer to perform my calculations using the Worksheet Function to have a better understanding of the code that is executing. Let's look at some more Worksheet Functions.

To calculate the Min Value in a range

```vba
Sub Find_Min()

Dim MinNum As Double

MinNum = WorksheetFunction.Min(Range("B1:B10"))

MsgBox ("The Minimum Value is " & MinNum)

End Sub
```

In the above example, the Minimum value is calculated from the range of cells from B1 to B10. The value is stored in the variable minimum.

The output of the above expression can be seen in the diagram below

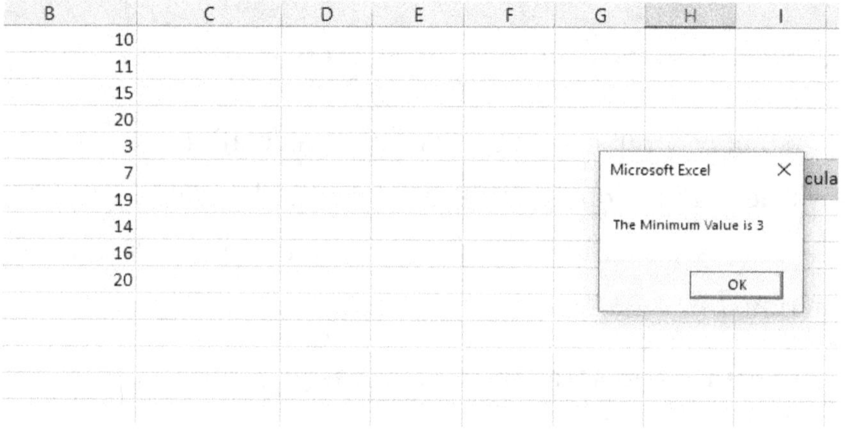

Similarly, you can also calculate the maximum value from the Range using the Max () function of the worksheet.

Vlookup Function

If you have ever interacted with an excel programmer, I am sure you must have heard about the Vlookup Function. You can never be an Excel Guru if you don't know how to implement the Vlookup Function. Vlookup is a potent function as it can help you the exact information from a table of any size. The Vlookup Function intakes four parameters. The first parameter represents the item that needs to be searched in the table. For example, in the below example, we are looking for product B. The second Parameter represents the range in which it needs to be looked up, the third parameter represents the column number that we want to return as a result, and finally, the four-parameter intakes a true or a false value. The true value tells the lookup to return a value that can be an approximate match, whereas the false value tells the lookup to only return a value when there is an exact match. In the following example, the user will be entering the product name in order to retrieve its price from the table. The product name will be entered using the Input Box Function. The price of the product will then be displayed on the output screen using the MsgBox Function.

```vba
Sub Get_Product_Price()

Dim Product

Dim Price As Integer

Product = InputBox("Enter the Product ")

Price = WorksheetFunction.VLookup(Product, Range("A2:D5"), 2, 0)

MsgBox ("The Product Price of " & Product & " is " & Price)

End Sub
```

As shown in the below diagram, the input box is prompted on the screen when the Macros is executed.

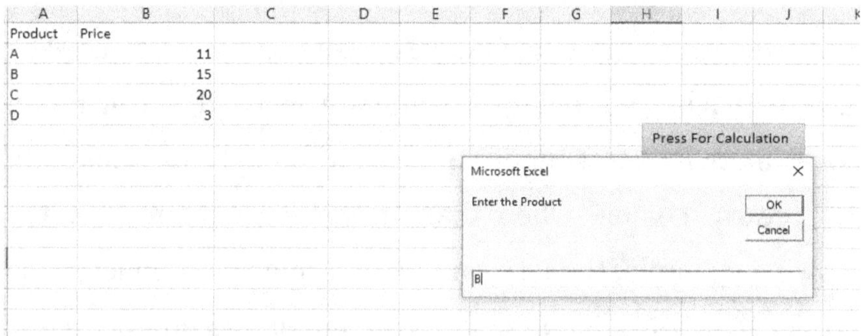

In the example, Product B was Entered. On pressing the Ok button, the Output was displayed.

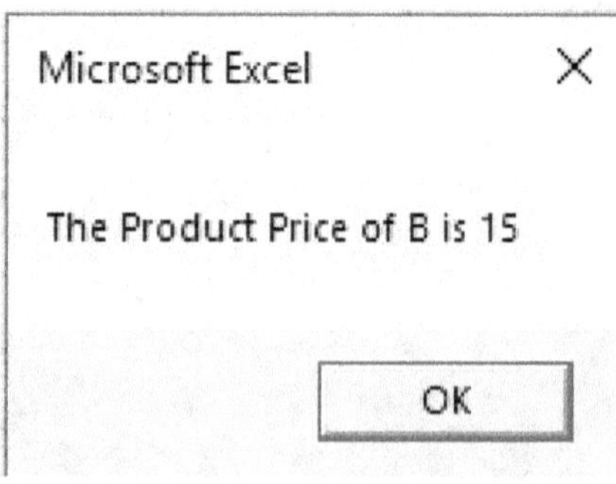

The Input was passed to the Vlookup Function. The Vlookup Function traversed Product B and returned the Price of the Product.

Chapter 4: Introduction to Pivot Tables

Pivot Tables are one of the most powerful features in Excel. They were invented in 1986 by Pito Salas, who was working for Lotus Corp at the time. It became more prominent in the early 1990s when Lotus Improv was released for the NeXT platform in 1991. It soon became one of the must-know features in Excel, especially if you are analysing large data sets. Before we delve into how to create pivot tables, it is important to know what it actually is.

What is a Pivot Table?

The pivot table is essentially a data summary tool that is created from a data source. You can summarise data in seconds by simply clicking and dragging fields from one area of the report to another. It can transform hundreds and thousands of rows and columns into meaningful information. You can display subtotals on any level of data you want. Arguably the biggest advantage of using pivot tables is in their interactivity. You can rearrange information without any effort. In fact, the reason why they are called pivot tables is that you can 'pivot' the data in any way you choose.

Why use Pivot Tables?

So why should you use a pivot table? The pivot table should be used if you want to summarise large amounts of data. If you try and summarise the information with Excel formulas, it will be

more time-consuming as you have to manually write the formulas. If you add more information to your data, then you may have to edit your formulas which can also be time-consuming. Pivot tables can easily be formatted to make them attractive and visually appealing, whereas, with manually created tables with formulas in, it can take longer to format. If you have a very large data set that is made up of hundreds of thousands of rows and columns, then using formulas to summarise your information will slow down the Excel calculation time. Whenever you make a change to your data, the formulas will take a while to recalculate. With a pivot table, you will not have any problems with slow calculation times.

Pivot Table Layout

There are four components of the pivot table which are contained in the pivot table Fields pane. The pivot table Fields is a task pane that is associated with the pivot table and, by default, is located on the right side of the window. The four components of the pivot table are:

1) Filters

2) Rows

3) Columns

4) Values

In the below screenshot, there are five fields (Product, Area, Month, Units, Sales). These are the column headings in the source data. Your pivot table appearance and information will be defined by what fields you enter in the four areas of the pivot table Fields pane. Now I will explain each area in turn.

Filters

Filters allow you to display just the data you want to see, and the rest of the data will be hidden. When you move a field in the Filters area, you can then choose which items in the field you want to see or not see by checking or unchecking the boxes. They work in the same way as a filter in a table. In the example below, the Area field is the filter.

Area	(All) ▾

Sum of Sales	Jan	Feb	Mar	Apr	May	Grand Total
Mouse			500			500
Mouse mat				134		134
PC		5600				5600
Printer	250					250
Scanner					540	540
Grand Total	250	5600	500	134	540	7024

Rows

Rows show each item in the field in separate rows. One field item occupies one row. They go down the left side of a pivot table. In the example below, the Product field is in the Rows area, and the items in the Product field are displayed in each row.

| Area | (All) | | | | | |

Sum of Sales						
	Jan	Feb	Mar	Apr	May	Grand Total
Mouse			500			500
Mouse mat				134		134
PC		5600				5600
Printer	250					250
Scanner					540	540
Grand Total	250	5600	500	134	540	7024

Columns

Columns show each item in the field across separate columns. In the example below, the Month field is in the Columns area, and each item in the Month field are in separate columns.

| Area | (All) | | | | | |

Sum of Sales						
	Jan	Feb	Mar	Apr	May	Grand Total
Mouse			500			500
Mouse mat				134		134
PC		5600				5600
Printer	250					250
Scanner					540	540
Grand Total	250	5600	500	134	540	7024

Values

Values show the summary information. In the example below, the Sales field is in the Values area. The pivot table below summarises the sales by-product in the different months. Excel offers many ways to summarise your information, such as SUM, COUNT, AVERAGE, MAX, MIN, and so on. You are required to enter at least one field in the Values area. You can have the same field in the Values area twice. For example, you can have the pivot table show the sum of sales and also the average sales by product and month.

| Area | (All) | | | | | |

Sum of Sales						
	Jan	Feb	Mar	Apr	May	Grand Total
Mouse			500			500
Mouse mat				134		134
PC		5600				5600
Printer	250					250
Scanner					540	540
Grand Total	250	5600	500	134	540	7024

Displaying the pivot table Fields Pane

Whenever you click on a pivot table, the pivot table Field pane will automatically appear. If for any reason it doesn't appear, then click any cell in the pivot table, and from the ribbon, click on the **Analyse** tab. Under the **Show,** group click on the **Field List** command button.

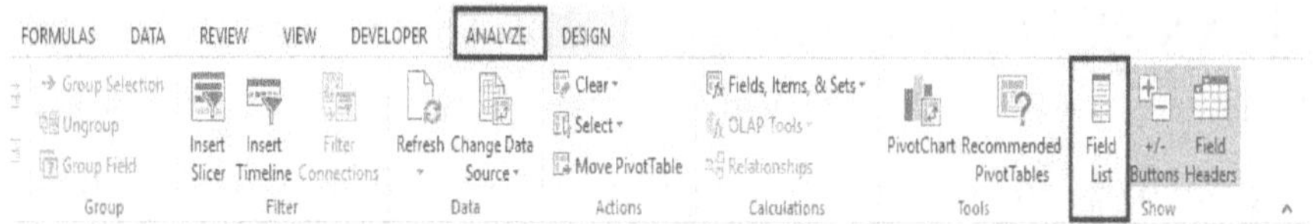

Structure of the Data Source

In order to create a pivot table, you need to ensure that your data source is structured correctly. This means your data must be rectangular in shape and stored in a worksheet range or a table. In order to change your worksheet range to a table, pick up a cell anywhere in the data and then from the ribbon, click on the **Insert** tab and, under the **Tables** group, select the **Table** command button.

The data to create a pivot tables needs to contain two types of fields:

1) **Data** – This is usually a value to be summarised. For example, the Sales field is the data field

2) **Category** – This describes the data. For example, the Product, Area, and Month fields are the category fields

It is also important to note that your data source must contain headings on all the columns; otherwise, you will get the below message.

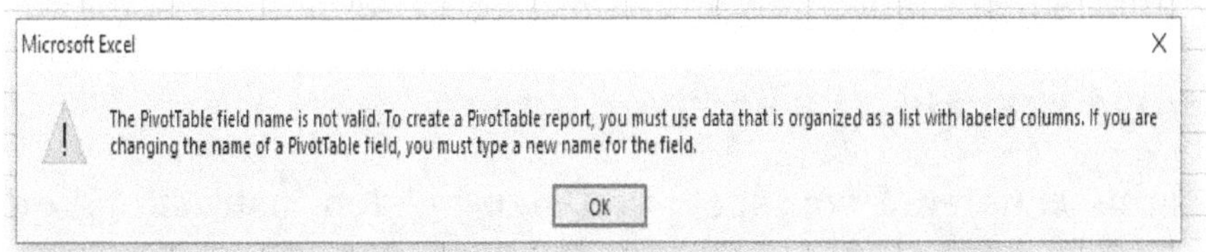

Updating Pivot Tables

Whenever you update the data source, the pivot table will not update immediately like with formulas. This is one of the downsides of using pivot tables instead of formulas. When you create a pivot table, Excel stores that data in a Pivot Cache. The Pivot Cache is automatically generated whenever you create a pivot table. It is like a container that stores the data source. Whenever you make changes to a pivot table, it doesn't use the data source but the Pivot Cache instead.

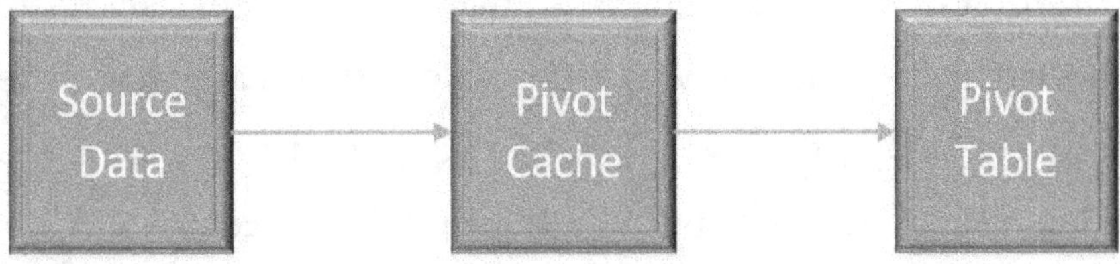

So why is there a Pivot Cache? Well, the Pivot Cache is there to optimize the functionality of a pivot table. It helps the pivot table summarise the information instantly whenever you drag and drop the fields in the Filters, Rows, Columns, and Values areas in the pivot table Fields pane.

This is the reason why the pivot table will not update straight away when you change the source data. In order to update the pivot table when the source data has changed, you must refresh a pivot table.

How to Create a Basic Pivot Table?

In this chapter, I will show you step-by-step instructions on how to create a pivot table.

Specifying the Source Data

The first thing you need to do is to specify what data you want to use to create a pivot table. To complete this, follow these instructions:

1) Select any cell in the data range. Tap on the **INSERT** tab in the ribbon, and then under the **Tables** group, select the **PivotTable** command button

2) The Create PivotTable dialog box will appear. Excel will attempt to specify the correct range of the data based on the active cell. If for any reason, Excel doesn't specify the correct range, then you can use your mouse to select the data range. In this example, I selected the range

A1:F22. The data range will appear in the **Table/Range** field

Specifying the Location of a pivot table

The next step is to specify where you want the pivot table to be located. You can specify whether to have the pivot table in a new worksheet or in the existing worksheet from the Create PivotTable dialog box. In this example, I have selected **New Worksheet**. If you want the pivot table in the existing worksheet, then select the **Existing Worksheet** and then specify the cell in the **Location** field. Once you have done this, click the **OK** button.

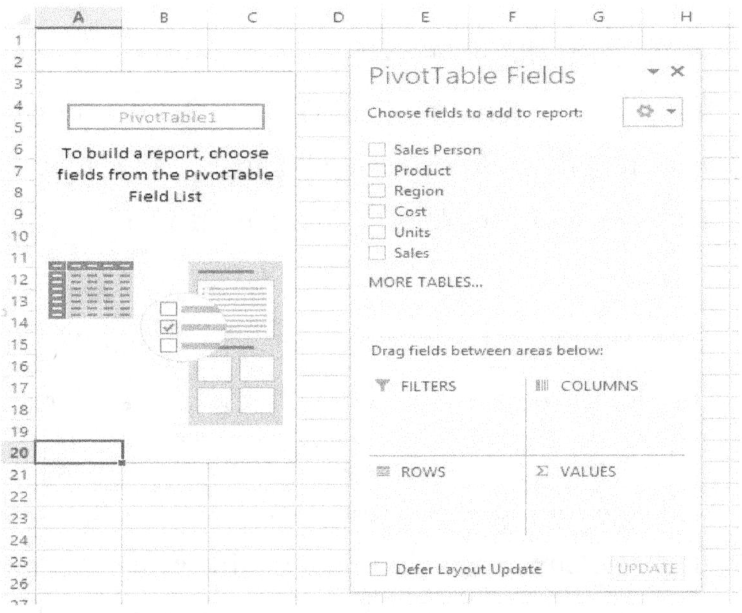

Adding Fields to a pivot table

You now need to build the pivot table by moving the fields in the Filters, Rows, Columns, and Values area of the pivot table Fields pane. In this example, I want to show the sales by product and sales person. You can move the fields into one of the four areas of the pivot table Fields pane by using one of the following methods:

1. Clicking and dragging the fields to one of the four areas.

2. Right-click the field name and choose one of the four areas in the shortcut menu. You can choose from Add to Report Filter, Add to Row Labels, Add to Column Labels or Add to Values. You can also add a field as a slicer.

1) Select the check box against the appropriate field. Excel will do its best to move it to the correct area. For example, when I checked the Sales Person field, it correctly moved it to the Rows area. Whenever you check the box for a field that contains values, then Excel will move it to the Values area. If Excel moves the field to an area you don't want it to be in, then you can simply do one of the first two options to move it to the correct area.

In the example below, I have created the pivot table that shows what furniture items each Sales person has sold along with the amount sold for each item. There is also a subtotal which shows the total sales sold by each Sales person.

The Sales person and Product fields are in the Rows area, and the Sales is in the Values area of the pivot table Fields pane.

Reorganizing a pivot table

Once you have created a pivot table, it is very easy to change it around to show different information. By pivoting the fields, you can answer different questions and look at different trends and patterns. To move the fields in a different area in the pivot table Fields pane, just click and drag the field to another area or right-click the field and select one of the options in the menu as described in the previous section. In this section, I will show you how easy it is to modify your pivot tables to show different summary information.

Show Sales for East Area Only

In the below example, I want to see all the sales for the East area only. For this, I put the Region field in the Filters area of the pivot table Fields pane. The filter will now display above a pivot table. I then just checked the East check box and unselected the other check boxes, and then pressed the OK button.

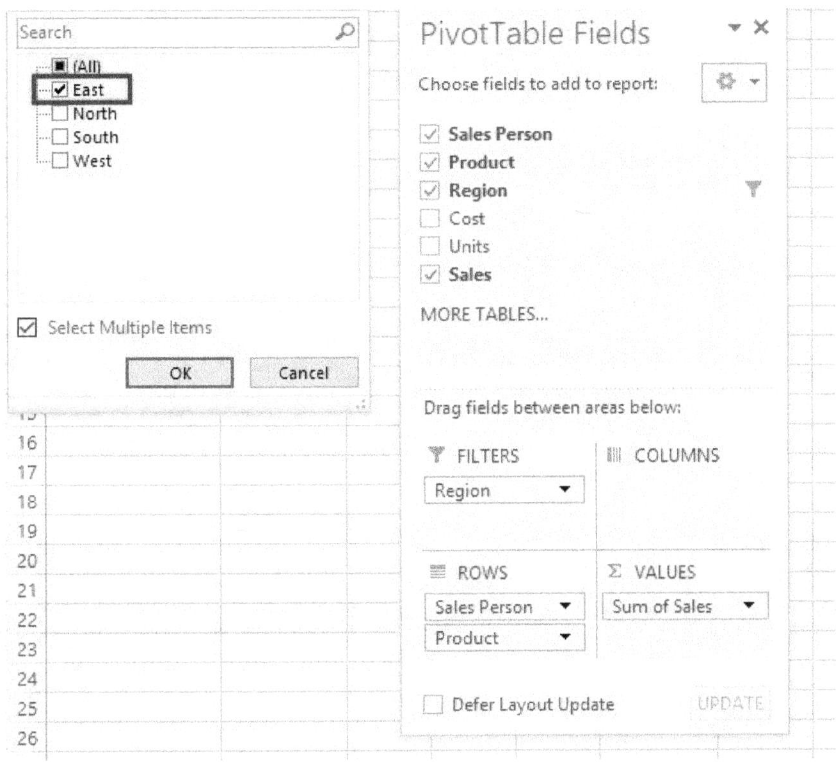

The pivot table now just displays information relating to the East area only.

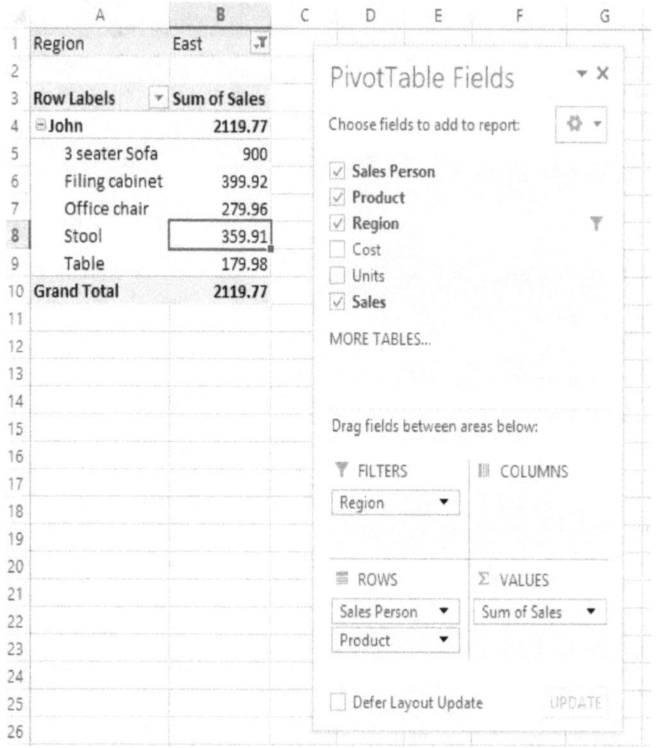

Show Total Sales by Furniture Item

In this example, I just want to see the total sales for each furniture item. I removed the Sales Person field by clicking it and dragging it away. The pivot table now displays the total sales for each furniture item. You can make this more meaningful by sorting the sales in descending order so you can easily see which furniture has made the most sales through to which has made the least sales.

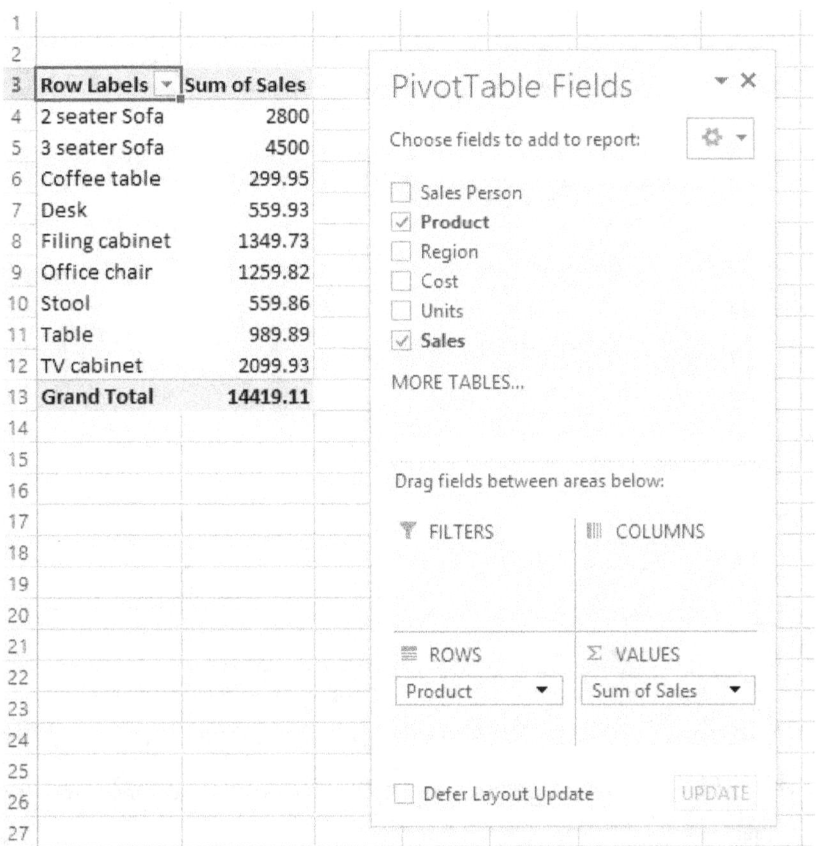

Show Sales by Area

In this example, I want to see what furniture items were sold in each area and see the total sales by area. I have put the Region field in the Columns area of the pivot table Fields pane, so each area is a column heading. The Product field is in the Rows area, so each furniture item occupies a row. The Sales is the Values area of the pivot table Fields pane.

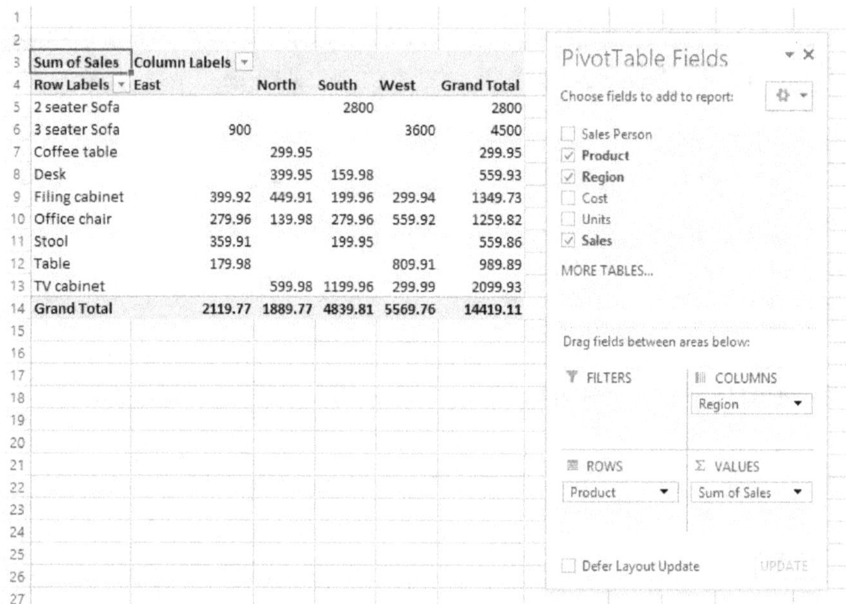

Show Total Sales Made by Sales Person

In this example, I want to see which Sales person has made the most sales. The Sales person is in the Rows area, and the Sales is in the Values area of the pivot table Fields pane. Again, to make this more meaningful, you would normally sort this in descending order of sales, so you get to see who the top Sales person is through to the Sales person who has made the least sales.

Refreshing a pivot table

As mentioned in the previous chapter, if the source data is updated, the pivot table will not automatically update. You need to update the pivot table by refreshing it to reflect the new changes. There are two ways to do this:

Method 1

From the ribbon, click the **Data** tab, and under the **Connections** group, click on the **Refresh All** command button.

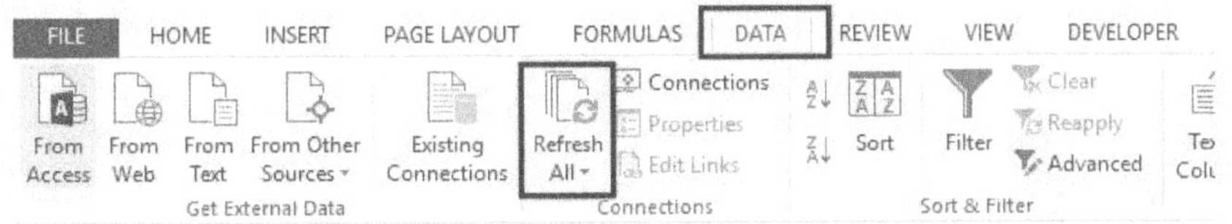

Method 2

Right-click any cell in the pivot table, and in the shortcut menu, select **Refresh**.

Changes to the Data Source

If your data source has changed and you have inserted new columns at the end, then the pivot table will not use these new columns unless you re-define the range.

	A	B	C	D	E	F	G	H	I
	Sales Person	Product	Region	Cost	Units	Sales	Sales Date	Month	Year
2	Jim	Desk	North	$79.99	5	$399.95	04/08/2019	Aug	2019
3	Sally	Office chair	South	$69.99	4	$279.96	05/08/2019	Aug	2019
4	Jim	Office chair	North	$69.99	2	$139.98	07/11/2019	Nov	2019
5	John	Filing cabinet	East	$49.99	8	$399.92	19/11/2019	Nov	2019
6	Lisa	Table	West	$89.99	9	$809.91	22/11/2019	Nov	2019
7	Sally	Filing cabinet	South	$49.99	4	$199.96	04/12/2019	Dec	2019
8	Lisa	3 seater Sofa	West	$900.00	4	$3,600.00	08/12/2019	Dec	2019
9	Jim	Filing cabinet	North	$49.99	9	$449.91	15/12/2019	Dec	2019
10	John	Table	East	$89.99	2	$179.98	21/12/2019	Dec	2019
11	Sally	2 seater Sofa	South	$700.00	4	$2,800.00	04/01/2020	Jan	2020
12	Lisa	Office chair	West	$69.99	8	$559.92	09/01/2020	Jan	2020
13	John	Stool	East	$39.99	9	$359.91	19/01/2020	Jan	2020
14	Jim	Coffee table	North	$59.99	5	$299.95	04/02/2020	Feb	2020
15	Sally	TV cabinet	South	$299.99	4	$1,199.96	08/02/2020	Feb	2020
16	Lisa	Filing cabinet	West	$49.99	6	$299.94	19/02/2020	Feb	2020
17	John	3 seater Sofa	East	$900.00	1	$900.00	06/03/2020	Mar	2020
18	Jim	TV cabinet	North	$299.99	2	$599.98	07/03/2020	Mar	2020
19	Sally	Stool	South	$39.99	5	$199.95	17/03/2020	Mar	2020
20	Lisa	TV cabinet	West	$299.99	1	$299.99	02/04/2020	Apr	2020
21	John	Office chair	East	$69.99	4	$279.96	28/04/2020	Apr	2020
22	Sally	Desk	South	$79.99	2	$159.98	07/05/2020	May	2020

To do this, follow these steps:

1) Click on a pivot table

2) In the ribbon, click on the **Analyse** tab, and under the **Data** group, click the **Change Data Source** command button

3) Excel will take you back to the data source, and the Change PivotTable Data Source dialog box will appear

4) You then select the range again, including the new columns in the

Table/Range field and then press the **OK** button

5) Refresh the pivot table as described in the previous section

6) The three new fields are now included in the pivot table Fields pane

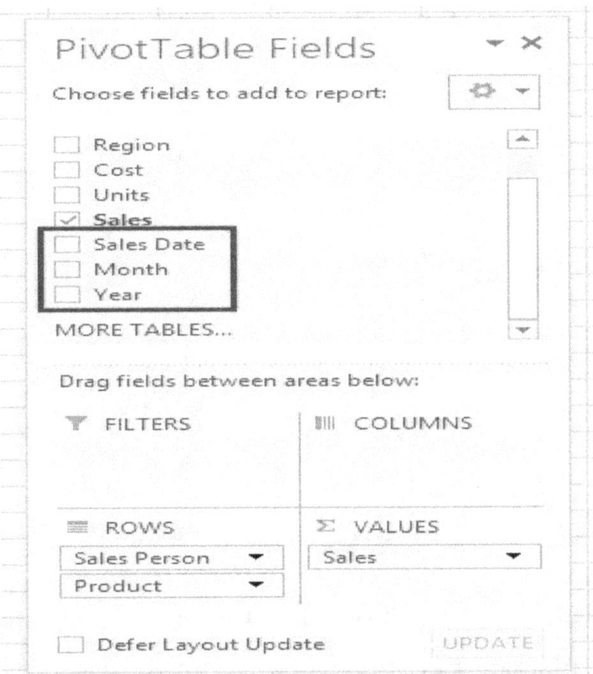

Changing the Calculation in the pivot table

By default, Excel will summarise the data in the pivot table by summing the values. You can change the calculation to show count, average, maximum value, minimum value, and so on. Here are the steps to change the calculation from Sum to Average:

1) Click any cell in the pivot table

2) Click on the field in the Values area of the pivot table Fields pane where you want to change the calculation. In this example, I click on the Sales field. From the menu select

Value Field Settings

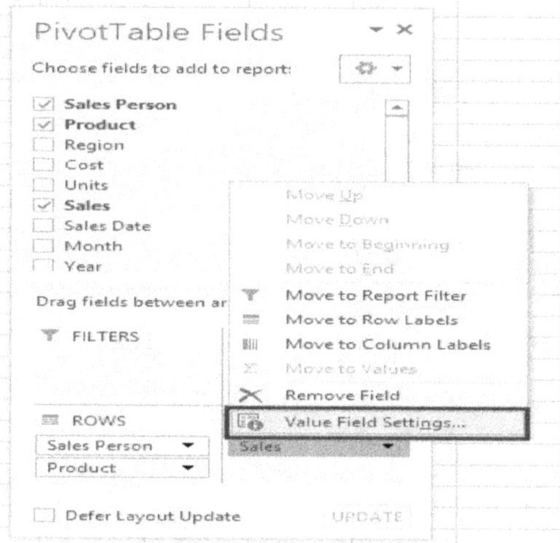

3) In the Value Field Settings dialog box, select the desired calculation under **Summarize value field**. In this example, I select **Average**. Once you have selected the calculation, click the **OK** button.

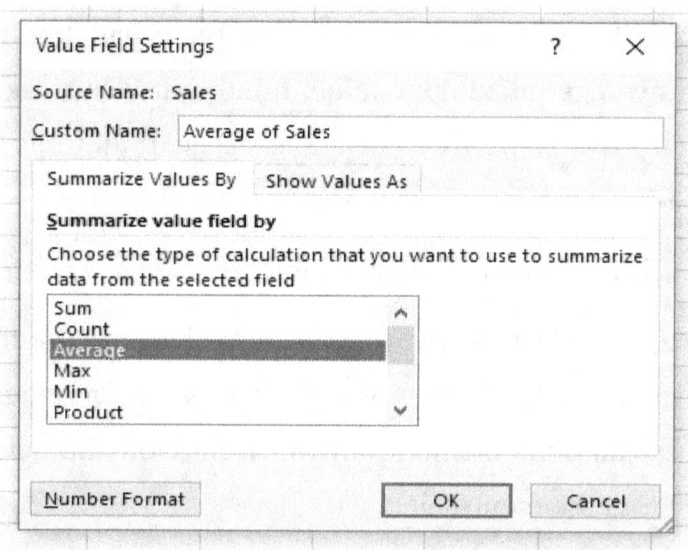

Customizing a pivot table

Now that I have taken you through the steps of how to create a pivot table, I will now show you how to customize the pivot table so it looks more professional, visually appealing, and easier to understand and interpret. There are various ways to customize and format pivot tables, and this chapter will explain how you can achieve this. I will use the same pivot table I created in the previous chapter.

Changing The style of pivot tables

Whenever you create a pivot table, Excel applies the default the style of pivot table. This looks dull and not very attractive to look at, especially if you are sending it to your manager or customer. Excel has many pivot tables styles which you can apply, so your pivot table stands out and looks more pleasing to the eye.

Here are the steps to apply the pivot table style:

1) Click a cell in the pivot table

2) Click the **Design** tab from the ribbon. In the **PivotTable Styles** group, click on the down arrow at the bottom right to see all the available styles you can choose from.

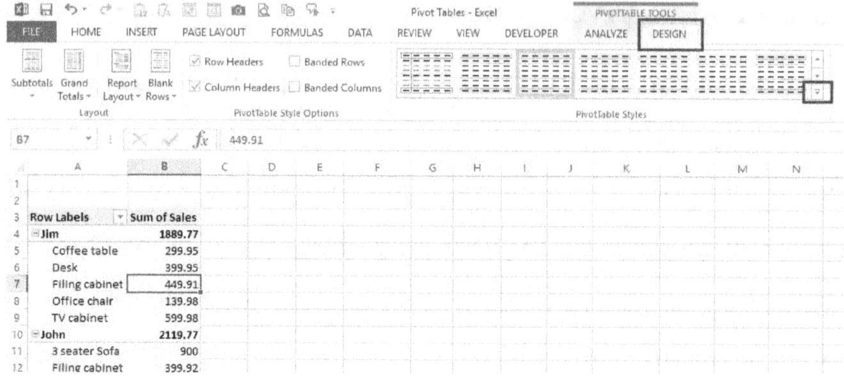

3) If you hover your mouse over the different the style of pivot tables, you can see the style being applicable to a pivot table. Once you are happy with a style, just click your left mouse button to apply it to a pivot table. In this example, I have selected 'Pivot Style Medium 2'.

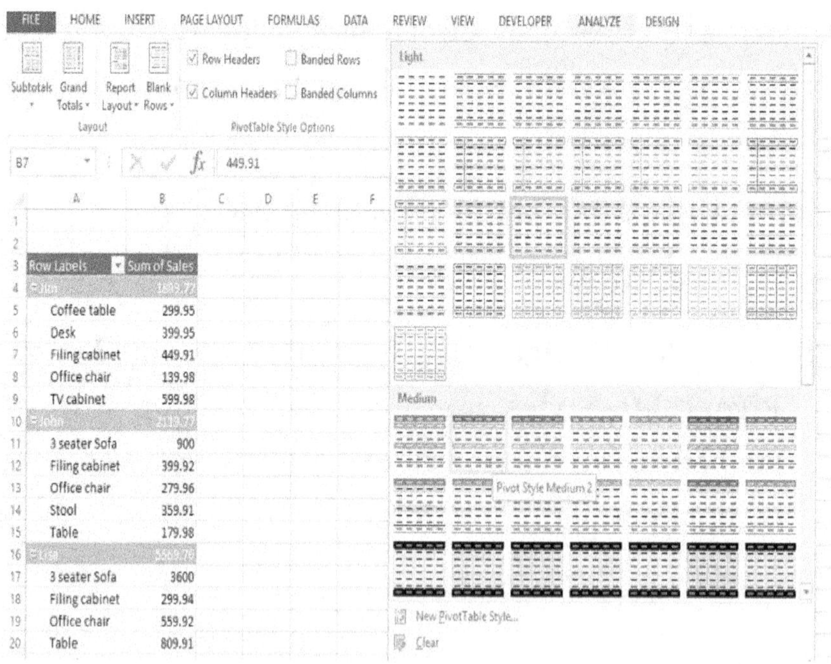

Create a New The style of pivot table

If you don't like any of the pivot table styles Excel has to offer, then you can create your own. For this example, I want to create the pivot table style that colours the pivot table grey and has a border around it. Here are the steps on how you can do this:

1) Select a cell in the pivot table

2) From the ribbon, click the **Design** tab. In the **PivotTable Styles,** group click on the down arrow, which is located on the bottom right

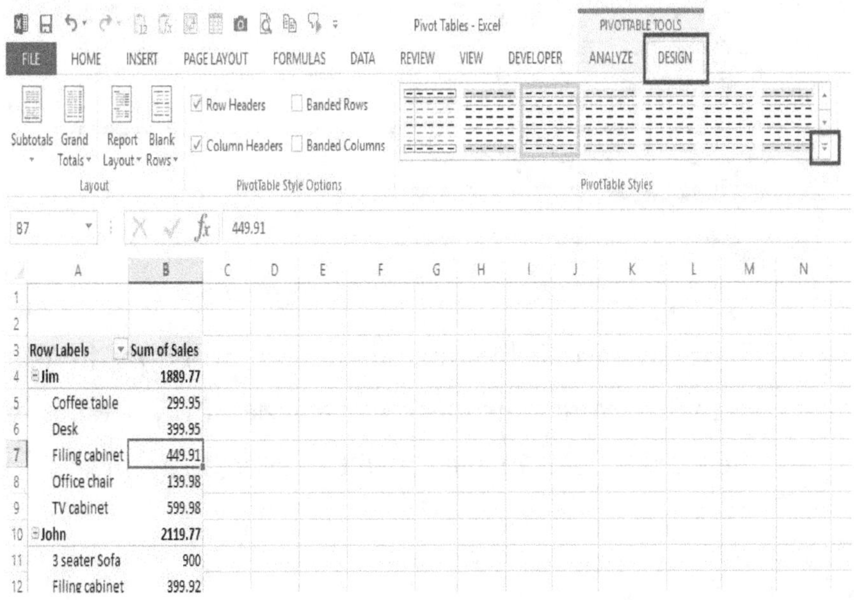

3) Select New PivotTable Style

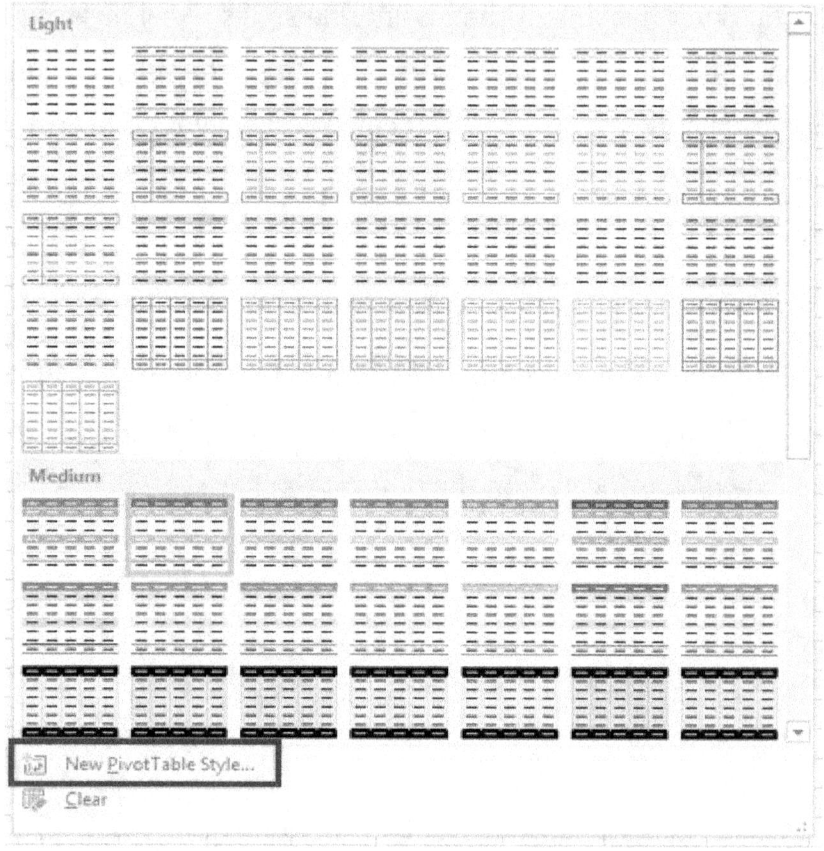

4) The New PivotTable Style dialog box will appear. You can name your new custom the style of pivot table in the **Name** field. I have called this style 'Example.'

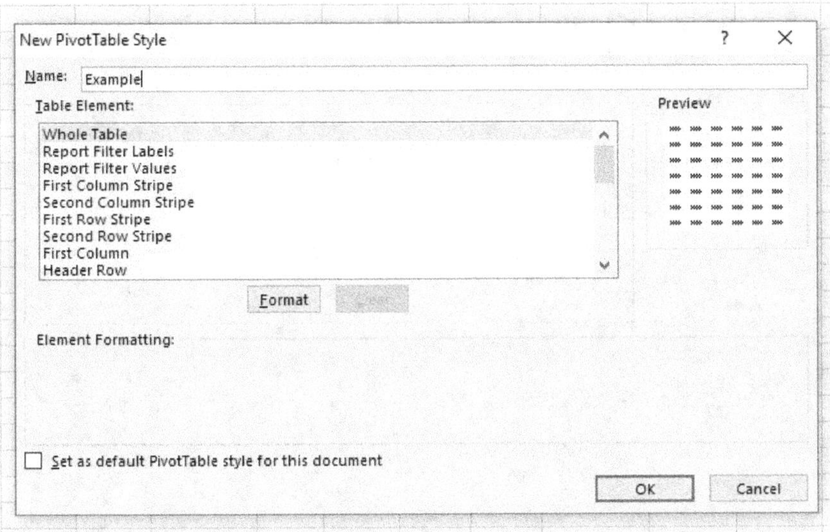

5) I want to make the whole pivot table grey and apply a border around it, so I select the **Whole Table** under **Table Element** and then select the **Format** button.

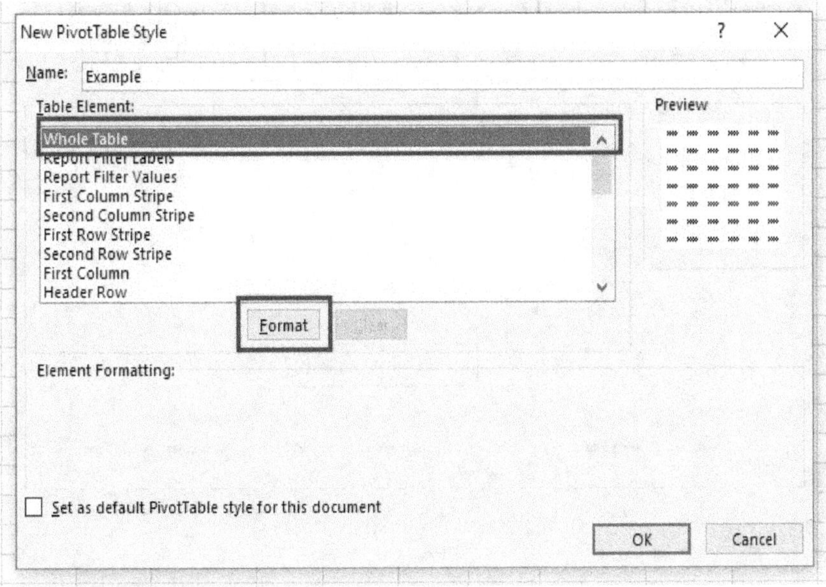

6) In the **Fill** tab, I select a grey colour

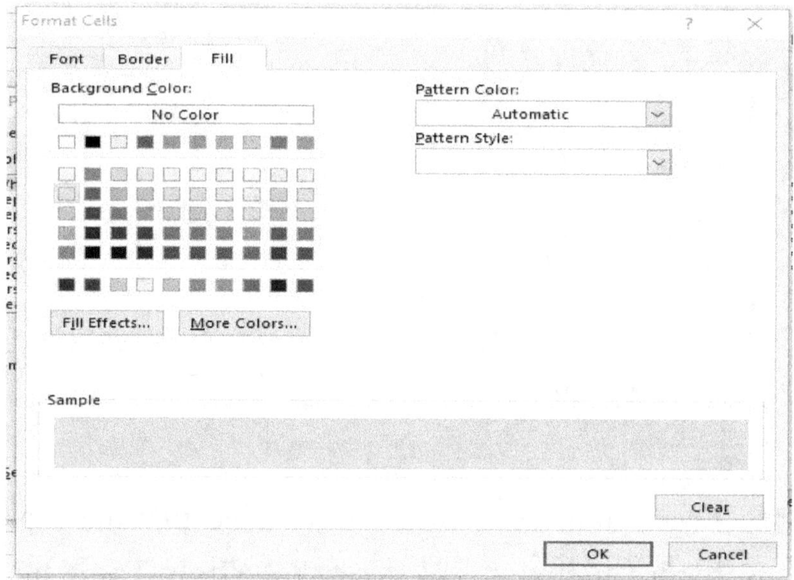

7) I then click on the **Border** tab and select a line style under the **Line Style** section and apply it in the **Border** section to all the edges. I then select **OK**

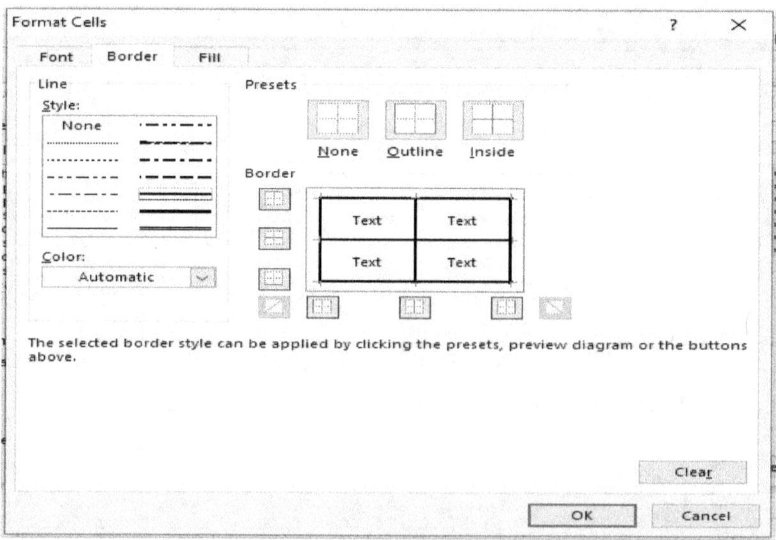

8) You will be taken back to the New PivotTable Style dialog box. You can see a preview of what the pivot table design will look like in the **Preview** section. Once you are happy, select **OK**

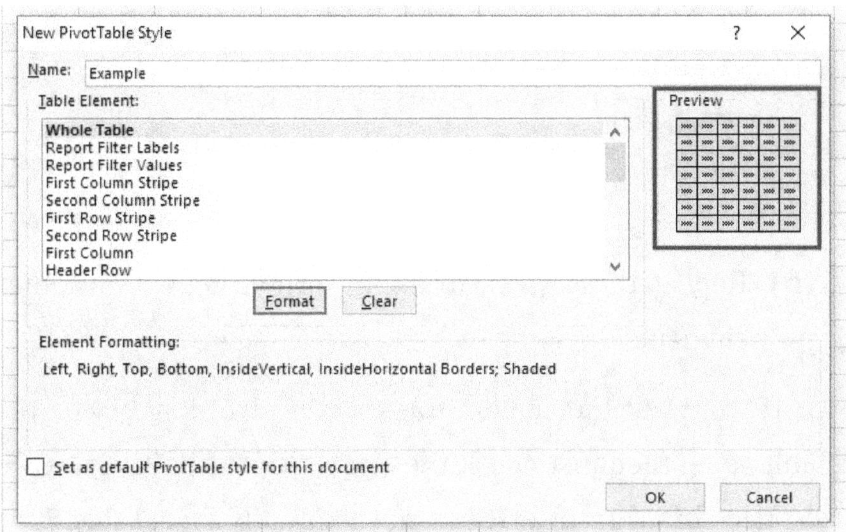

9) To apply this new custom the style of pivot table, click on the **Design** tab in the ribbon, and under the **PivotTable Styles** group, click on the down arrow to open up the pivot table styles as explained in step 2. Your newly created the style of pivot table will be located under the **Custom** heading. Click your left mouse button to apply your custom style to a pivot table

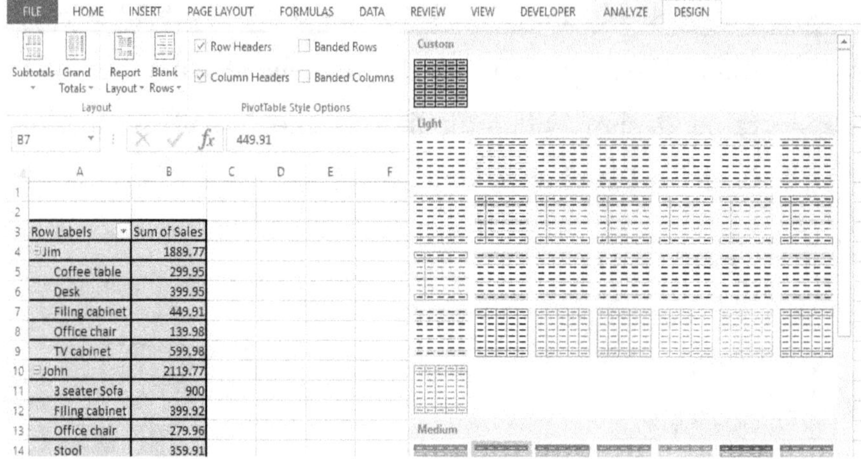

10) Repeat these steps to apply formatting to any other elements

Tip: If you want the custom the style of pivot table to be the default style, then just check the **Set as default PivotTable style for this document** box in the Modify PivotTable Style dialog box.

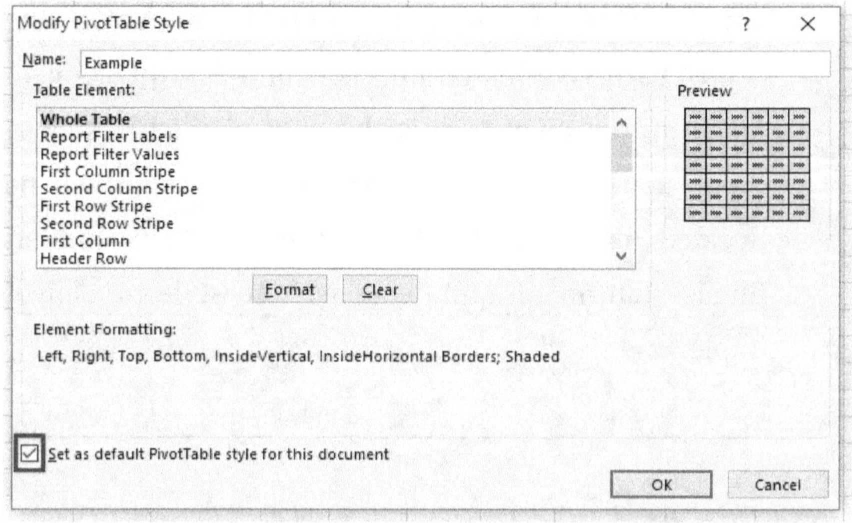

The style of pivot table Options

You can apply further the style of pivot table options in the **PivotTable Style Options** group. This is located in the **Design** tab in the ribbon.

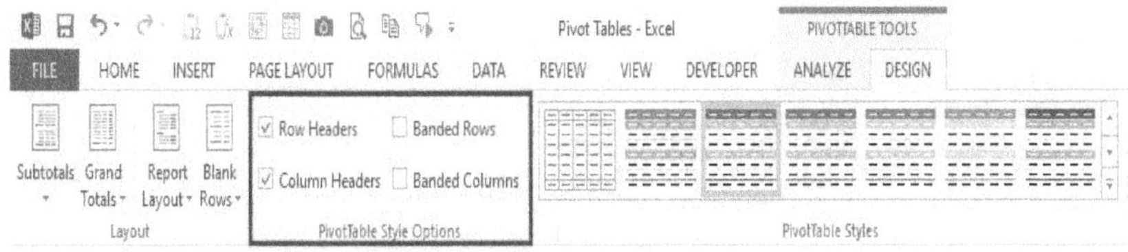

There are four options to choose from:

1) **Row Headers** – This adds or removes shading to the row headers depending on whether you select this option or not

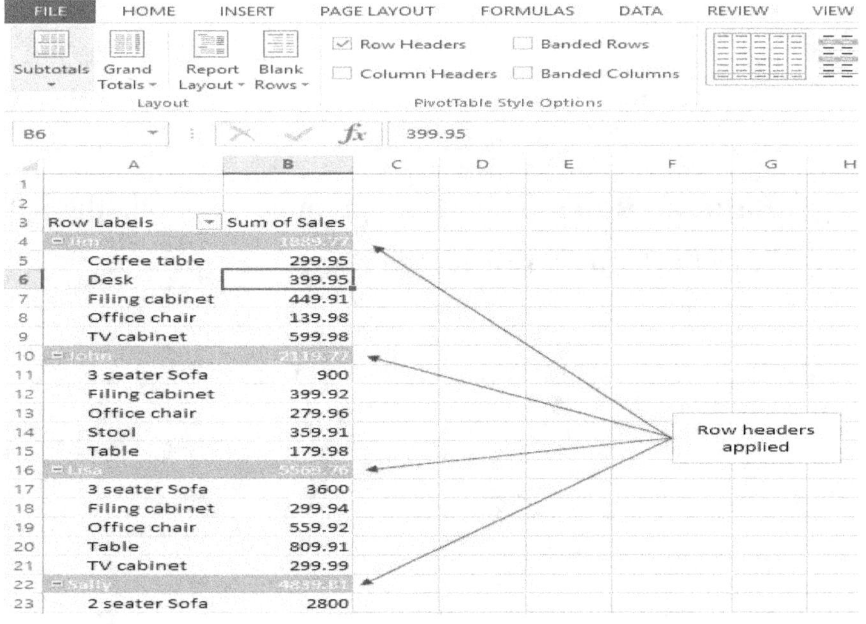

2) Column Headers – This adds or removes shading to the column header depending on if this option is selected or not.

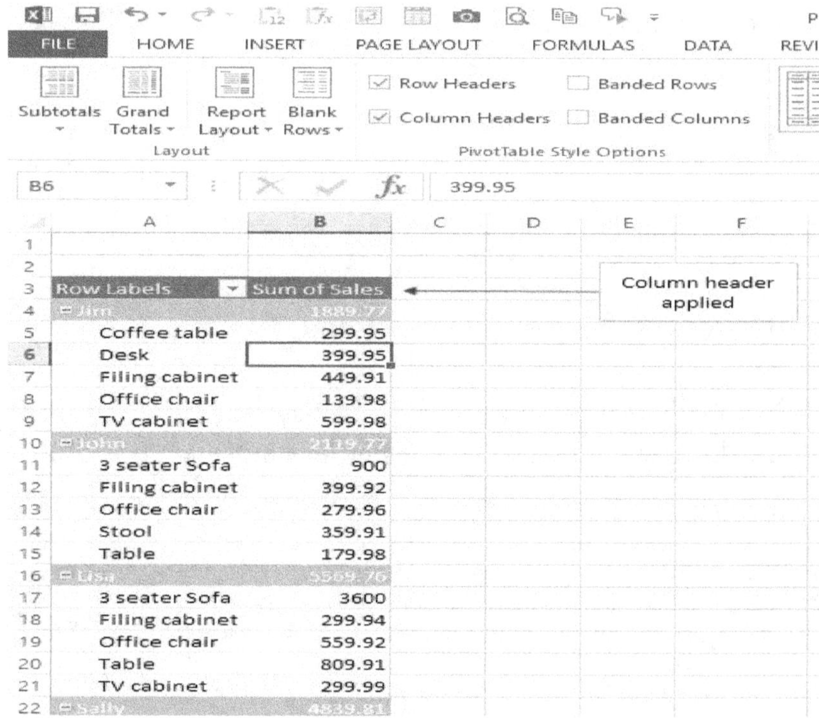

3) Banded Rows – If this option is selected, then it applies a thick line between each row

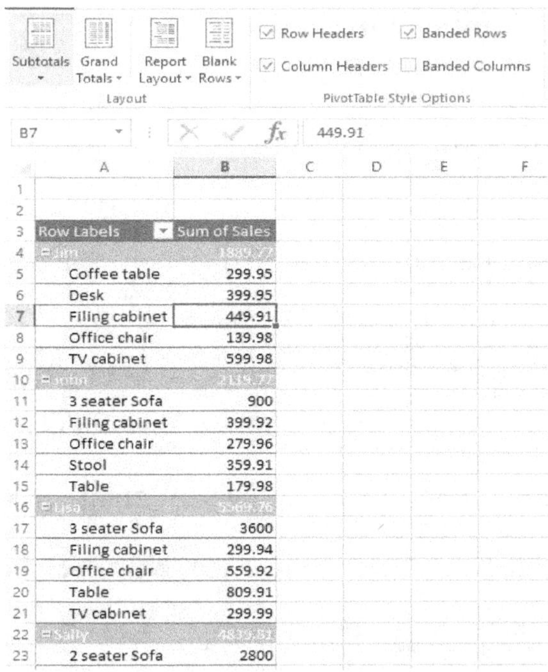

4) Banded Columns - If this option is selected, then it applies a thick line between each column

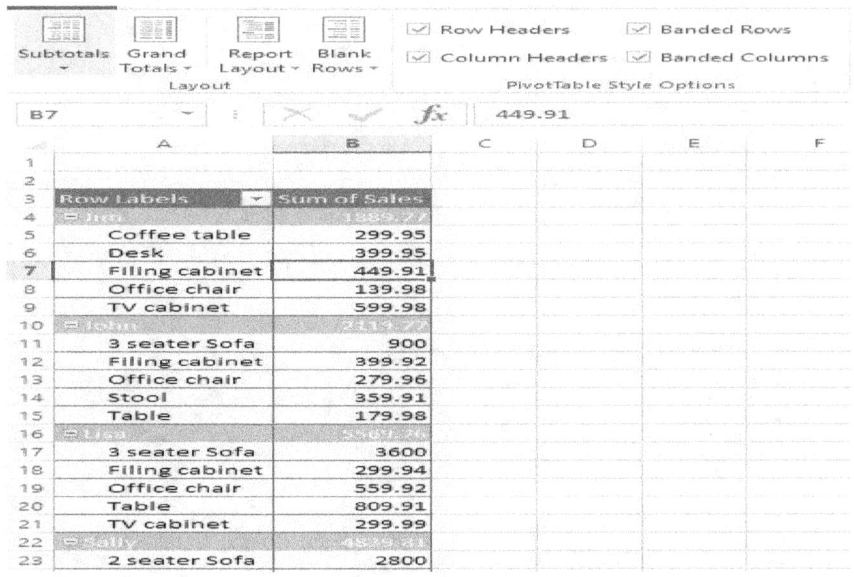

Applying Number Formatting

To make your pivot tables more meaningful, you can apply number formatting to the values. For example, you can apply different currencies, decimal places, date formats, percentages, and so on. The pivot table I have created so far contains just values under the Sales column. We don't know what these values actually mean. In this example, I will show you the steps to change the values to US dollars.

1) Select a cell in the pivot table and right-click the mouse

2) From the shortcut menu, select **Number Format**

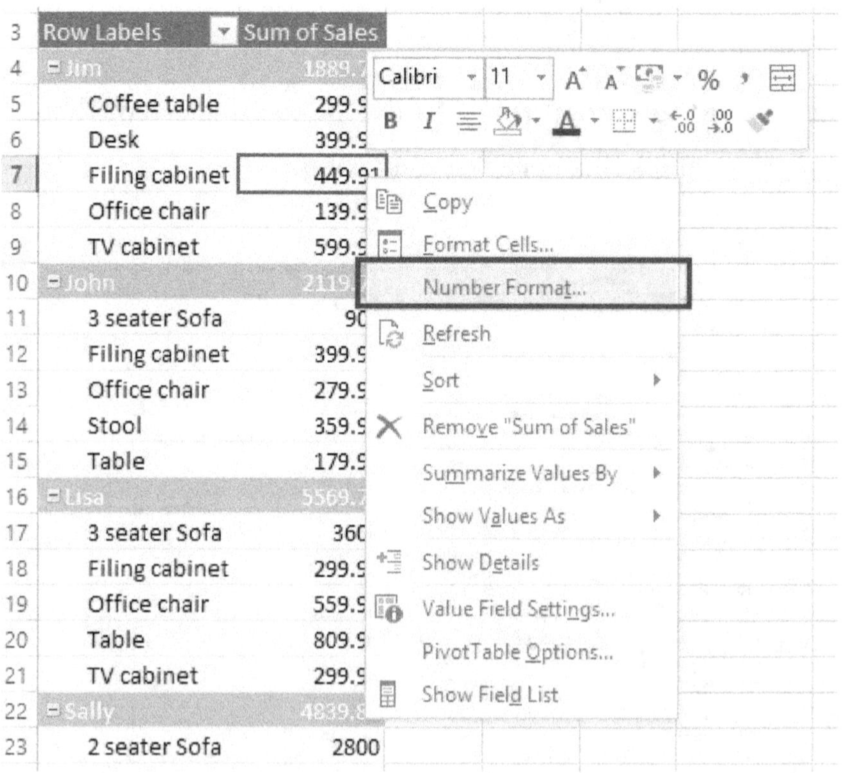

3) In the Format Cells dialog box, select **Currency** under **Category**. Select a currency symbol from the drop-down menu in the **Symbol** field. In this example, I selected **$ English (United States)**. You can also choose how many decimal places you want in the **Decimal Places** field. The default is 2 decimal places, and in this example, I have left it at 2. Once you are happy with your selections, then press the **OK** button.

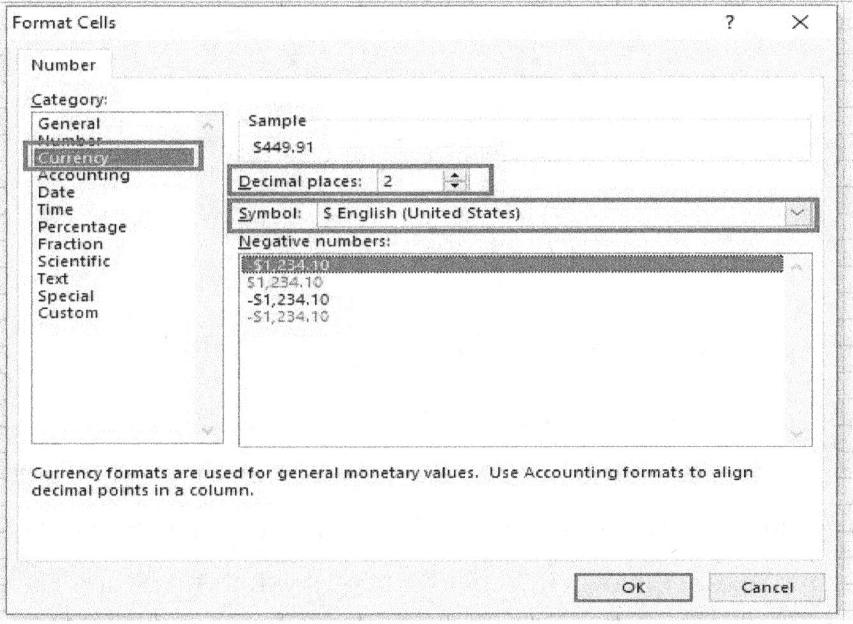

4) The sales are now in US dollars

	A	B
1		
2		
3	Row Labels	Sum of Sales
4	⊟ Jim	$1,889.77
5	Coffee table	$299.95
6	Desk	$399.95
7	Filing cabinet	$449.91
8	Office chair	$139.98
9	TV cabinet	$599.98
10	⊟ John	$2,119.77
11	3 seater Sofa	$900.00
12	Filing cabinet	$399.92
13	Office chair	$279.96
14	Stool	$359.91
15	Table	$179.98
16	⊟ Lisa	$5,569.76
17	3 seater Sofa	$3,600.00
18	Filing cabinet	$299.94
19	Office chair	$559.92
20	Table	$809.91
21	TV cabinet	$299.99
22	⊟ Sally	$4,839.81
23	2 seater Sofa	$2,800.00

Move Field Position in the pivot table Field Pane

You may want to change the look of your pivot table, so it shows information in a different way. You can move fields up or down, so they are located in different positions. For example, the pivot table below shows what furniture each Sales person has sold and the sales amount. The Sales Person field is in the first position, and the Product field is in the second position in the Rows area of the pivot table Fields pane.

	A	B	C
2			
3	Row Labels ▼	Sum of Sales	
4	⊟ Jim	$1,889.77	
5	Coffee table	$299.95	
6	Desk	$399.95	
7	Filing cabinet	$449.91	
8	Office chair	$139.98	
9	TV cabinet	$599.98	
10	⊟ John	$2,119.77	
11	3 seater Sofa	$900.00	
12	Filing cabinet	$399.92	
13	Office chair	$279.96	
14	Stool	$359.91	
15	Table	$179.98	
16	⊟ Lisa	$5,569.76	
17	3 seater Sofa	$3,600.00	
18	Filing cabinet	$299.94	
19	Office chair	$559.92	
20	Table	$809.91	
21	TV cabinet	$299.99	
22	⊟ Sally	$4,839.81	
23	2 seater Sofa	$2,800.00	
24	Desk	$159.98	

I now want to move the Product field in the first position in the Rows area, so it is above the Sales Person field. There are two ways to do this:

1) Clicking and dragging the field and moving it to the first position in the Rows area. In this example, I would click and drag the Product field and move it above the Sales Person field

2) Clicking the field and from the shortcut menu select **Move up**. In this example, I would click the Product field and select **Move up,** which will move the field above the Sales Person field

Notice the dynamic of the pivot table has changed, and the main row headers are the furniture items and not the Sales people.

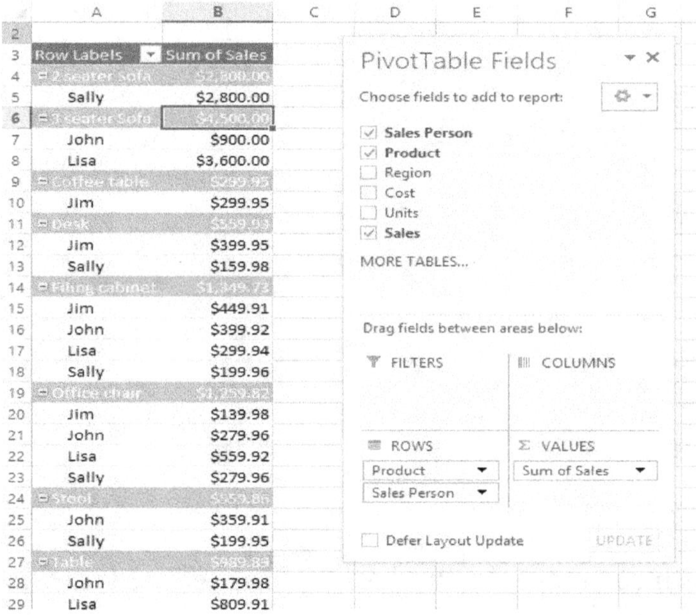

You can change the field positions back again using the same methods above.

Change Pivot Table Headings

You may want to give your pivot table headings more suitable names. By default, the row headings are called 'Row Labels,' column headings are called 'Column Labels', and the value headings start with 'Sum of' if the calculation to summarise the values is SUM. It would be called 'Count of' if the calculation is count, 'Average of' if an average is used as the calculation, and so on.

Row Labels	Sum of Sales
Jim	[illegible]
Coffee table	$299.95
Desk	$399.95
Filing cabinet	$449.91
Office chair	$139.98
TV cabinet	$599.98
John	[illegible]
3 seater Sofa	$900.00
Filing cabinet	$399.92
Office chair	$279.96
Stool	$359.91
Table	$179.98
Lisa	[illegible]
3 seater Sofa	$3,600.00
Filing cabinet	$299.94
Office chair	$559.92
Table	$809.91
TV cabinet	$299.99
Sally	[illegible]
2 seater Sofa	$2,800.00
Desk	$159.98
Filing cabinet	$199.96
Office chair	$279.96
Stool	$199.95

To change a pivot table's headings is simple. Just select the pivot tableheading you want to change and, in the Formula bar, type the new heading name. In this example, I have named the row heading 'Sales Person' and the values heading 'Sales by Sales Person.'

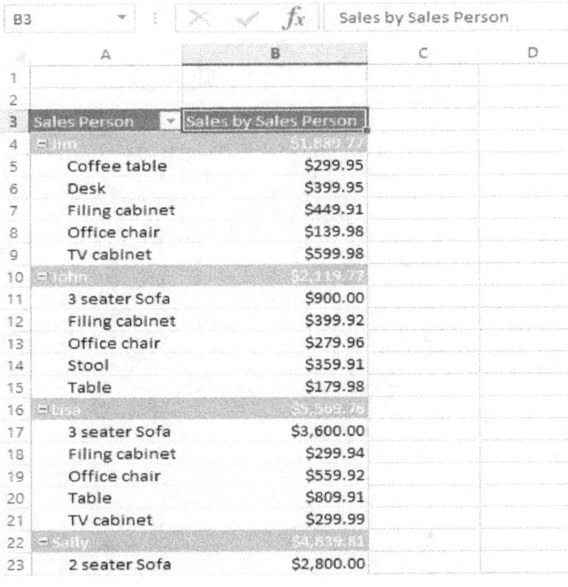

B3	f_x	Sales by Sales Person

	A	B	C	D
1				
2				
3	Sales Person	Sales by Sales Person		
4	Jim	$1,889.77		
5	Coffee table	$299.95		
6	Desk	$399.95		
7	Filing cabinet	$449.91		
8	Office chair	$139.98		
9	TV cabinet	$599.98		
10	John	$2,119.77		
11	3 seater Sofa	$900.00		
12	Filing cabinet	$399.92		
13	Office chair	$279.96		
14	Stool	$359.91		
15	Table	$179.98		
16	Lisa	$5,569.76		
17	3 seater Sofa	$3,600.00		
18	Filing cabinet	$299.94		
19	Office chair	$559.92		
20	Table	$809.91		
21	TV cabinet	$299.99		
22	Sally	$4,639.81		
23	2 seater Sofa	$2,800.00		

Tip: You cannot name the pivot table heading the same name as a field name. For example, if I tried to name the values heading 'Sales,' I would get the following message because there is a field name in the Values area already called 'Sales.'

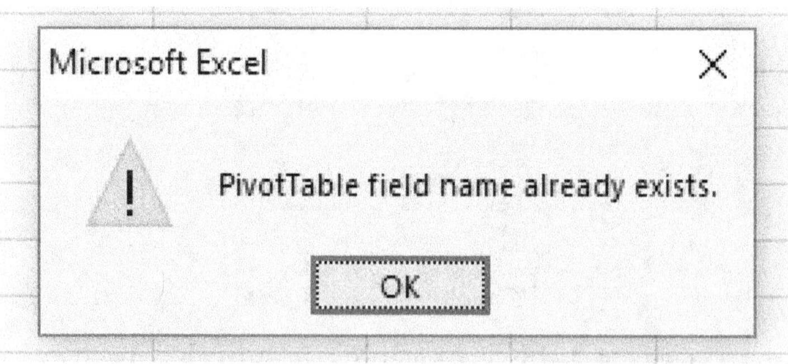

You can over-ride this by adding a space after the heading name. Excel sees space as a character, so it will see the heading and the field name as two different names.

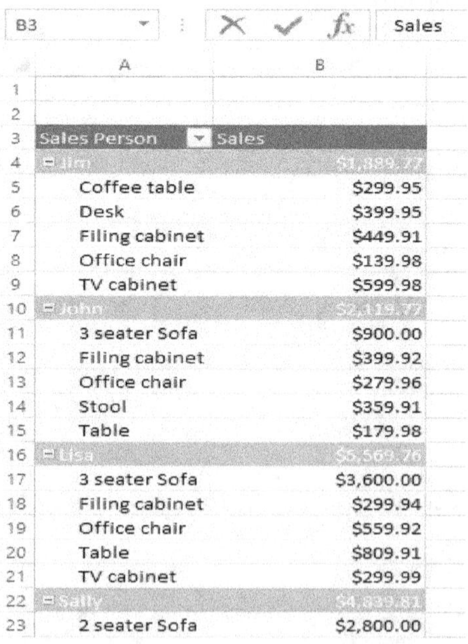

Changing Report Layout

A report layout is how the pivot table lays out the information and how it looks. When you create a pivot table, the default setting is Compact Form. Excel offers three different layouts; which you can choose from once you have created a pivot table. I will explain each layout in more detail.

1) **Compact Form** – This is used when you want to save spreadsheet space and reduce pivot table width. Each pivot table field in the Row area of the pivot table Fields pane is slightly indented from the one above to differentiate the fields. The field rows cannot be repeated.

2) **Outline Form** – This is used when you are not concerned about spreadsheet space, and you want to display each field. Each field in the Rows area of the pivot

table Fields pane are in separate columns. Row labels can also be repeated.

	Sales Person	Product	Sales
3	Sales Person ▼	Product ▼	Sales
4	⊟ Jim		$1,889.77
5		Coffee table	$299.95
6		Desk	$399.95
7		Filing cabinet	$449.91
8		Office chair	$139.98
9		TV cabinet	$599.98
10	⊟ John		$2,119.77
11		3 seater Sofa	$900.00
12		Filing cabinet	$399.92
13		Office chair	$279.96
14		Stool	$359.91
15		Table	$179.98
16	⊟ Lisa		$5,569.76
17		3 seater Sofa	$3,600.00
18		Filing cabinet	$299.94
19		Office chair	$559.92
20		Table	$809.91
21		TV cabinet	$299.99
22	⊟ Sally		$4,839.81
23		2 seater Sofa	$2,800.00
24		Desk	$159.98

3) Tabular Form – This is the most common layout as it is the easiest to read. The fields in the Rows area of the pivot table Fields pane are in separate columns, and the row labels can be repeated. The subtotals are also in separate rows.

	Sales Person	Product	Sales
3	Sales Person ▼	Product ▼	Sales
4	⊟ Jim	Coffee table	$299.95
5		Desk	$399.95
6		Filing cabinet	$449.91
7		Office chair	$139.98
8		TV cabinet	$599.98
9	Jim Total		$1,889.77
10	⊟ John	3 seater Sofa	$900.00
11		Filing cabinet	$399.92
12		Office chair	$279.96
13		Stool	$359.91
14		Table	$179.98
15	John Total		$2,119.77
16	⊟ Lisa	3 seater Sofa	$3,600.00
17		Filing cabinet	$299.94
18		Office chair	$559.92
19		Table	$809.91
20		TV cabinet	$299.99
21	Lisa Total		$5,569.76
22	⊟ Sally	2 seater Sofa	$2,800.00
23		Desk	$159.98
24		Filing cabinet	$199.96

To change the report layout, follow these steps:

1) Select a cell in the pivot table

2) Click the **Design** tab from the ribbon, and then under the **Layout** group, click on the **Report Layout** command button

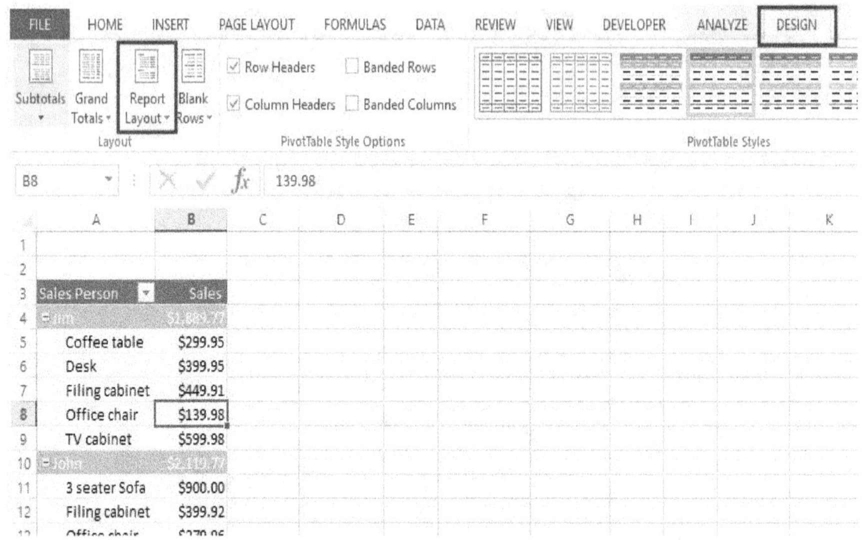

3) Select the desired report layout from the menu

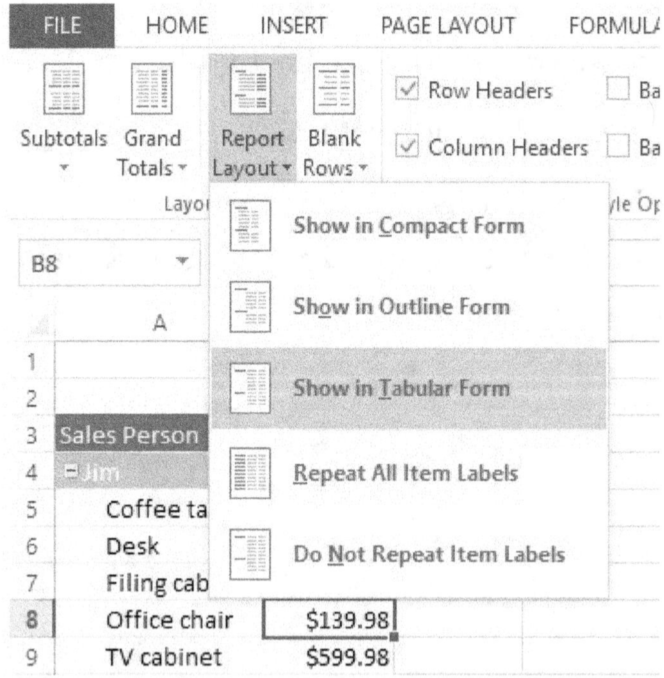

4) In this example, I selected **Tabular Form**

	Sales Person	Product	Sales
2			
3	Sales Person	Product	Sales
4	Jim	Coffee table	$299.95
5		Desk	$399.95
6		Filing cabinet	$449.91
7		Office chair	$139.98
8		TV cabinet	$599.98
9	Jim Total		$1,889.77
10	John	3 seater Sofa	$900.00
11		Filing cabinet	$399.92
12		Office chair	$279.96
13		Stool	$359.91
14		Table	$179.98
15	John Total		$2,119.77
16	Lisa	3 seater Sofa	$3,600.00
17		Filing cabinet	$299.94
18		Office chair	$559.92
19		Table	$809.91
20		TV cabinet	$299.99
21	Lisa Total		$5,569.76
22	Sally	2 seater Sofa	$2,800.00
23		Desk	$159.98

Repeat Item Labels

When you select the Outline or Tabular Form layout, you can repeat the item labels. This means item labels are repeated in each row. By default, they are not repeated.

To repeat item labels, select a cell in the pivot table. From the ribbon, click the **Design** tab, and under the **Layout** group, click the **Report Layout** command button. From the menu, select **Repeat All Item Labels**.

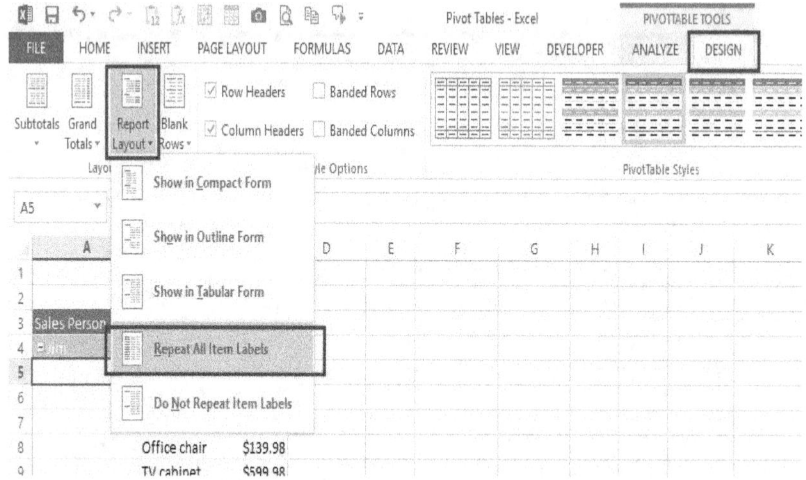

The item labels are now repeated.

If you do not want to repeat item labels, simply select **Do Not Repeat Item Labels**.

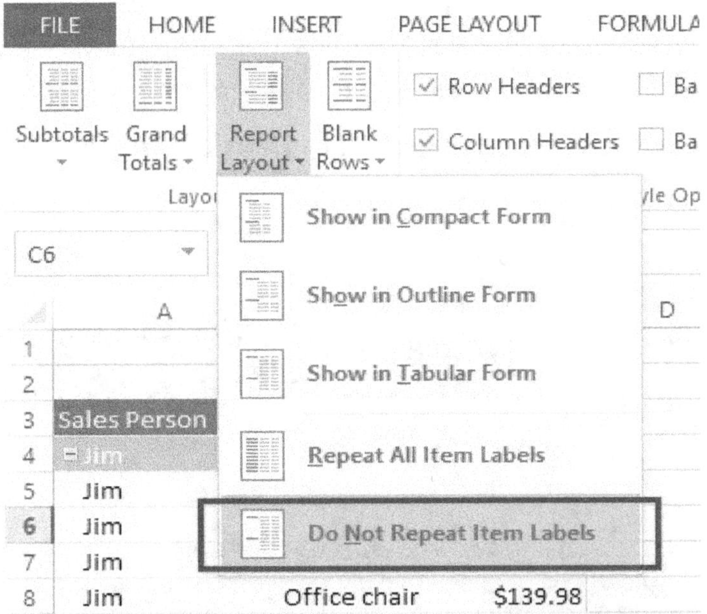

Displaying Grand Totals

You can choose to display or turn off grand totals in your pivot table. There are four settings to choose from:

1) **Off for Rows and Columns** - This turns off the grand totals for each row and column

2) **On for Rows and Columns** - This turns on the grand totals for each row and column

3) **On for Rows Only** – This displays the grand totals for each row but not for each column

4) **On for Columns Only** – This displays the grand totals for each column but not for each row

Here are the steps to apply grand totals to a pivot table:

1) Select any cell in the pivot table

2) In the ribbon, select the **Design** tab, and under the **Layout,** group select the **Grand Totals** command button

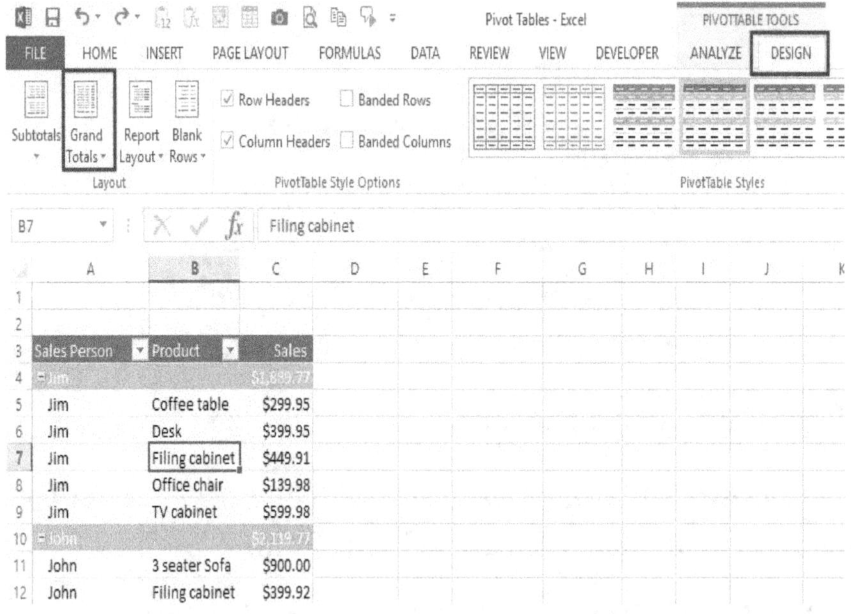

3) Choose from the list of options in the menu. In this example, I have chosen **On for Rows and Columns**

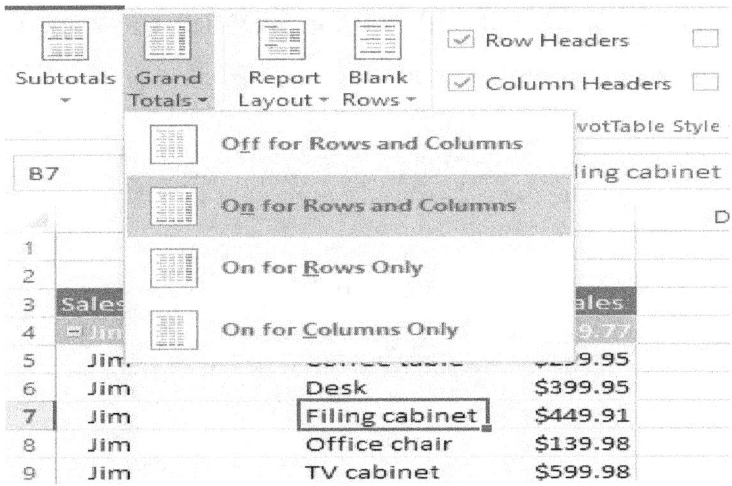

Displaying Subtotals

Like with grand totals, you can also display or turn off subtotals. There are three settings to choose from:

1) Do not Show Subtotals – This turns off subtotals

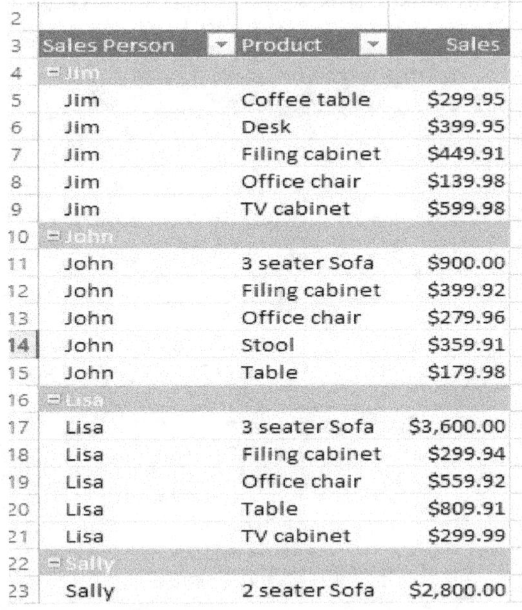

2) Show all Subtotals at the bottom of Group – This displays all subtotals at the bottom of each group

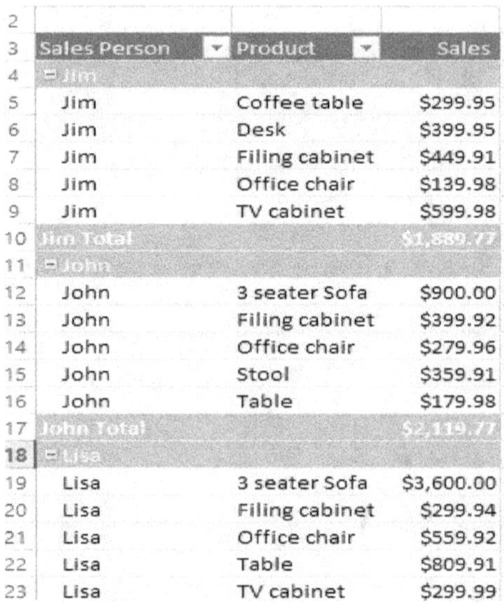

Sales Person	Product	Sales
Jim		
Jim	Coffee table	$299.95
Jim	Desk	$399.95
Jim	Filing cabinet	$449.91
Jim	Office chair	$139.98
Jim	TV cabinet	$599.98
Jim Total		$1,889.77
John		
John	3 seater Sofa	$900.00
John	Filing cabinet	$399.92
John	Office chair	$279.96
John	Stool	$359.91
John	Table	$179.98
John Total		$2,119.77
Lisa		
Lisa	3 seater Sofa	$3,600.00
Lisa	Filing cabinet	$299.94
Lisa	Office chair	$559.92
Lisa	Table	$809.91
Lisa	TV cabinet	$299.99

3) Show all Subtotals at the top of Group – This displays all subtotals at the top of each group

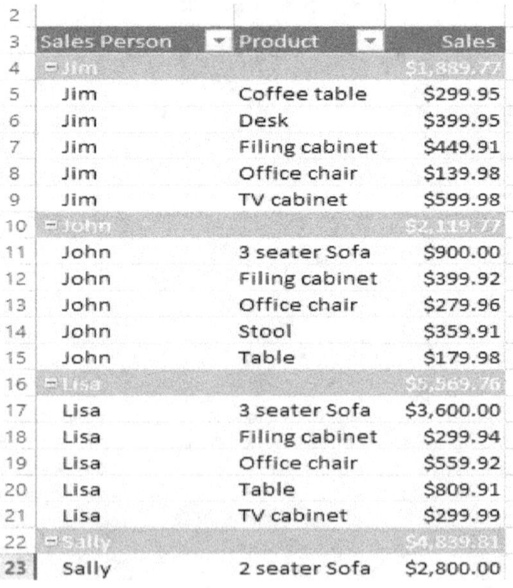

Sales Person	Product	Sales
Jim		$1,889.77
Jim	Coffee table	$299.95
Jim	Desk	$399.95
Jim	Filing cabinet	$449.91
Jim	Office chair	$139.98
Jim	TV cabinet	$599.98
John		$2,119.77
John	3 seater Sofa	$900.00
John	Filing cabinet	$399.92
John	Office chair	$279.96
John	Stool	$359.91
John	Table	$179.98
Lisa		$5,569.76
Lisa	3 seater Sofa	$3,600.00
Lisa	Filing cabinet	$299.94
Lisa	Office chair	$559.92
Lisa	Table	$809.91
Lisa	TV cabinet	$299.99
Sally		$4,839.81
Sally	2 seater Sofa	$2,800.00

Here are the steps to apply subtotals to a pivot table:

1) Select any cell in the pivot table

2) In the ribbon, select the **Design** tab, and under the **Layout,** group select the **Subtotals** command button

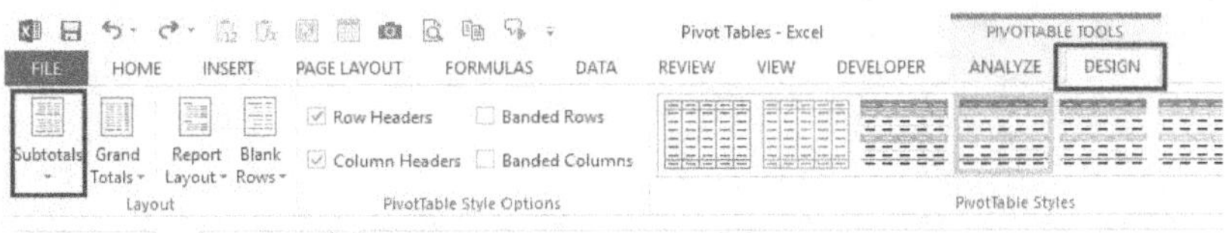

3) Choose from the list of options. In this example, I have chosen **Show all Subtotals at the top of Group**

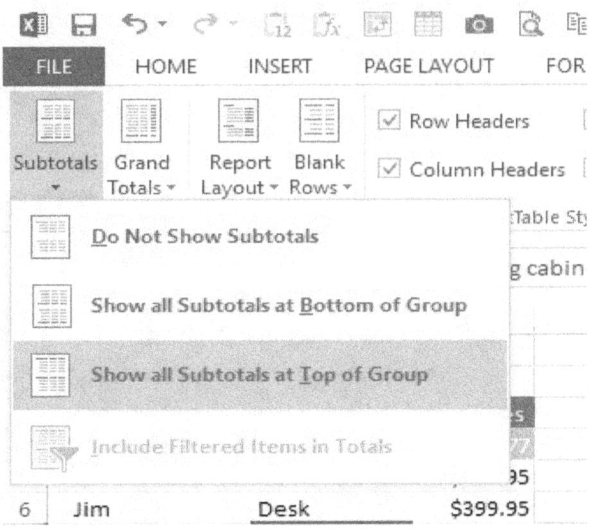

Inserting Blank Rows in the pivot table

To make your pivot table more visually appealing and easier to read, you can insert blank rows after each row item. Here are the steps to insert the blank rows:

1) Click on a cell in the pivot table

2) From the ribbon, click the **Design** tab, and under the **Layout,** group select the **Blank Rows** command button

3) Select Insert Blank Line after Each Item from the menu

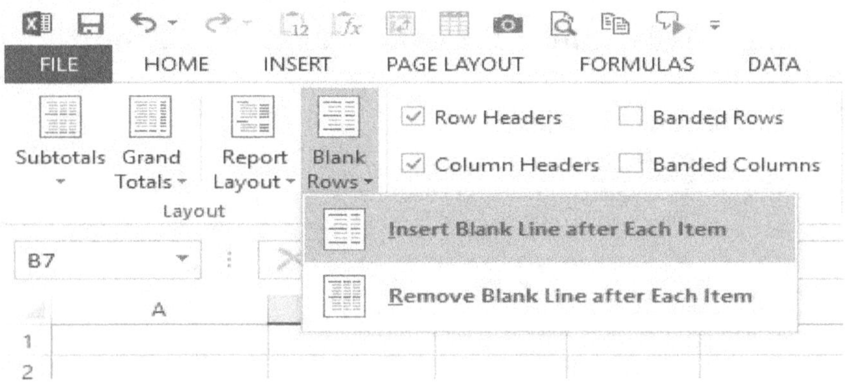

4) A blank line is now inserted after each row item

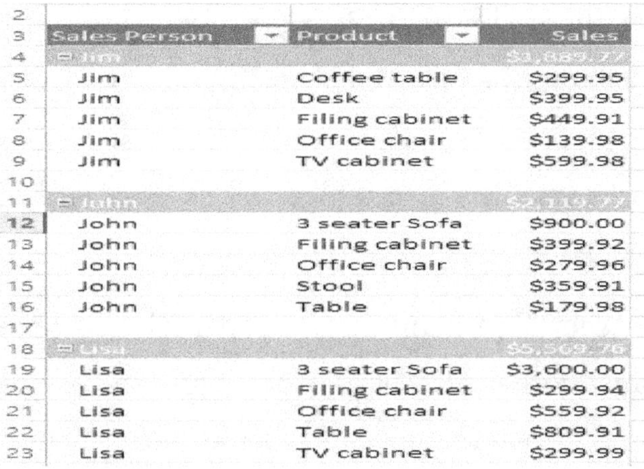

5) To remove the blank rows, just repeat steps 1 and 2, but this time, select

Remove Blank Line after Each Item

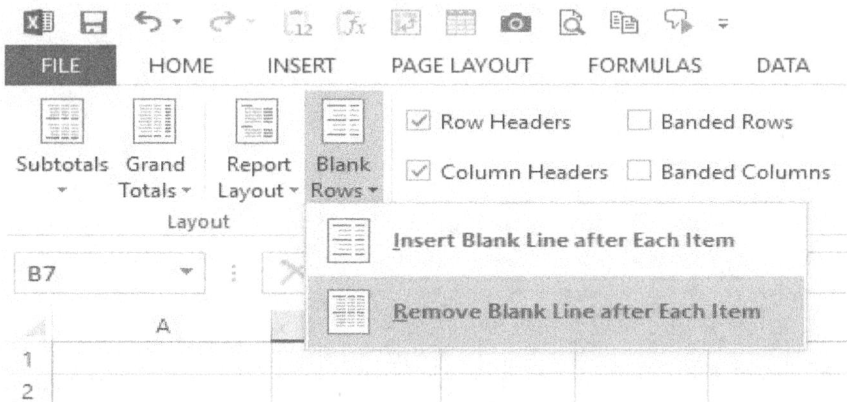

Replace Blank Cells with Zeros in the pivot table

Whenever there is no data in a row or column in the source data, by default, the pivot table will show a blank cell. This can make the pivot table look incomplete and messy. A nice tidy way to overcome this is to replace blank cells with zeros in the pivot table. Now let's look at how to do this.

Cell C6 is therefore blank in the pivot table as shown below. This means there is no record of sales for the desk by Jim. It is good practice to show any no sales as zero so that it doesn't look incomplete and is consistent with the other cells in the pivot table as they all contain numbers.

	A	B	C	D
1				
2				
3	Sales Person ▼	Product ▼	Sales	
4	⊟ Jim		$1,489.82	
5		Coffee table	$299.95	
6		Desk		
7		Filing cabinet	$449.91	
8		Office chair	$139.98	
9		TV cabinet	$599.98	
10	⊟ John		$2,119.77	
11		3 seater Sofa	$900.00	
12		Filing cabinet	$399.92	
13		Office chair	$279.96	
14		Stool	$359.91	
15		Table	$179.98	
16	⊟ Lisa		$5,569.76	
17		3 seater Sofa	$3,600.00	
18		Filing cabinet	$299.94	

To show zeros instead of blank cells, follow these instructions:

1)   Right-click any cell in the pivot table, and from the shortcut menu, select

PivotTable Options

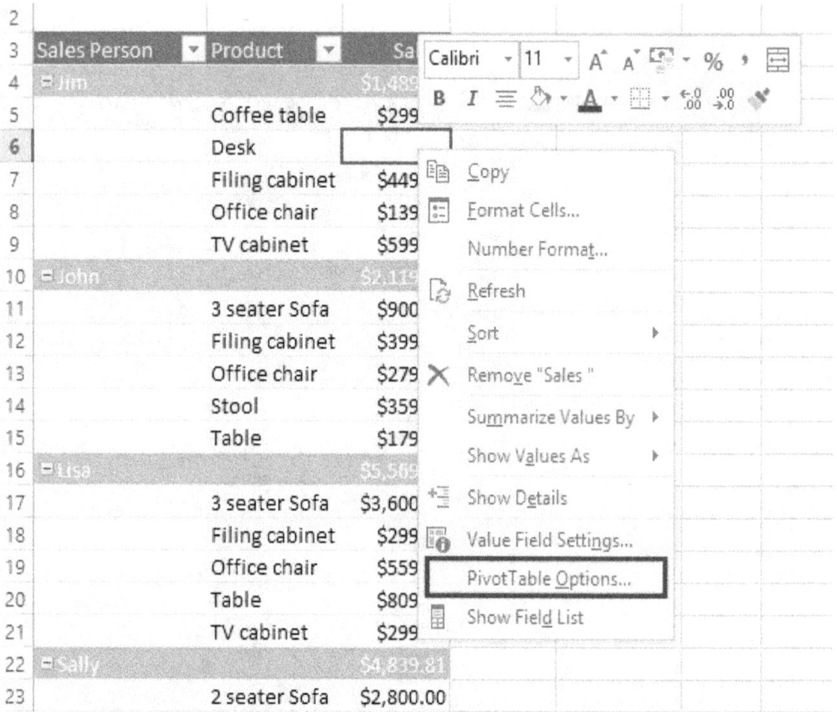

2) In the PivotTable Options, the dialog box selects the **Layout & Format** tab. Under the **Format,** section make sure the **For empty cells show** box is checked and enter a 0 in the field and then click the **OK** button

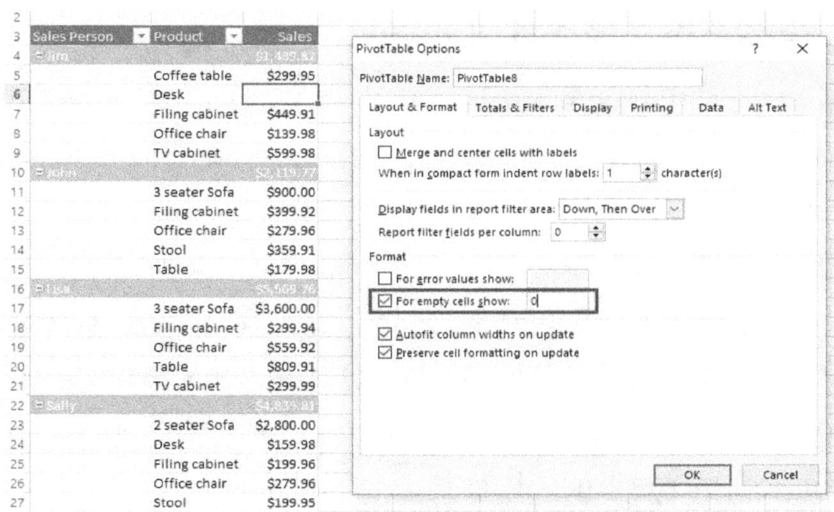

3) Cell C6 now shows $0.00

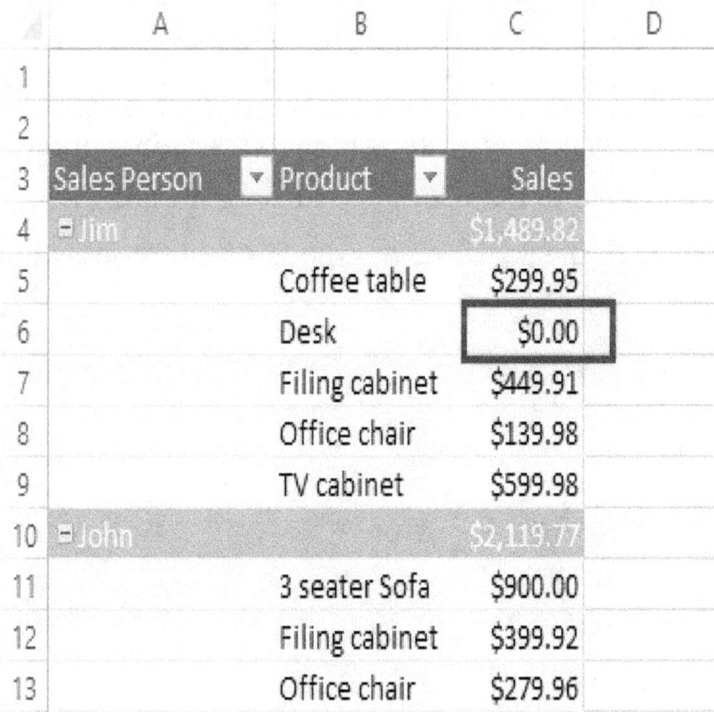

Sorting, Filtering, and Grouping

Pivot tables offer additional features such as sorting, filtering, and grouping. Sorting the pivot table helps you to visualize the information easier, for example sorting the rows in alphabetical order or sorting values in descending or ascending order. Filtering helps you to view certain information and hide the information you don't want to see. Grouping helps you to organize your pivot table better. For example, you can group dates by year and month.

Sorting a Pivot Table

You sort the pivot table in the same way as sorting data in an Excel worksheet. The below pivot table shows the total sales by each Sales person. As you can see, the pivot tableis not in any particular order. I want to sort this pivot table in descending order of sales, so I know who the top-performing Sales person is through to the Sales person who has sold the least amount.

	A	B	C
3	Sales Person	Product	Sales
4	Jim		$1,889.77
5		Coffee table	$299.95
6		Desk	$399.95
7		Filing cabinet	$449.91
8		Office chair	$139.98
9		TV cabinet	$599.98
10	John		$2,119.77
11		3 seater Sofa	$900.00
12		Filing cabinet	$399.92
13		Office chair	$279.96
14		Stool	$359.91
15		Table	$179.98
16	Lisa		$5,569.76
17		3 seater Sofa	$3,600.00
18		Filing cabinet	$299.94
19		Office chair	$559.92
20		Table	$809.91
21		TV cabinet	$299.99
22	Sally		$4,839.81
23		2 seater Sofa	$2,800.00
24		Desk	$159.98
25		Filing cabinet	$199.96
26		Office chair	$279.96
27		Stool	$199.95
28		TV cabinet	$1,199.96
29	Grand Total		$14,419.11

To sort a pivot table, follow these steps:

1) Click one of the cells that contain the subtotal. In this example, I select cell C4

	A	B	C
3	Sales Person	Product	Sales
4	= Jim		$1,889.77
5		Office chair	$139.98
6		Coffee table	$299.95
7		Desk	$399.95
8		Filing cabinet	$449.91
9		TV cabinet	$599.98
10	= John		$2,119.77
11		Table	$179.98
12		Office chair	$279.96
13		Stool	$359.91
14		Filing cabinet	$399.92
15		3 seater Sofa	$900.00
16	= Lisa		$5,569.76
17		Filing cabinet	$299.94
18		TV cabinet	$299.99
19		Office chair	$559.92
20		Table	$809.91
21		3 seater Sofa	$3,600.00
22	= Sally		$4,839.81
23		Desk	$159.98
24		Stool	$199.95
25		Filing cabinet	$199.96

2) In the ribbon, click on the **Data** tab, and under the **Sort & Filter** group, click the **Sort Z to A** command button

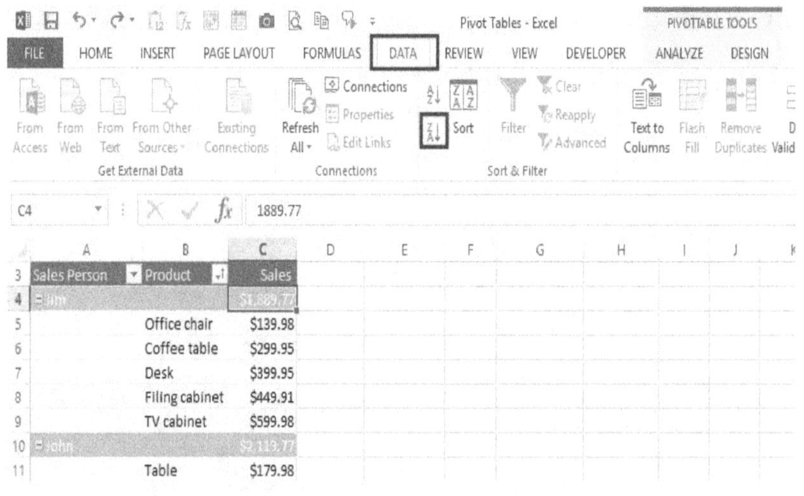

3) The pivot tableis now sorted by sales. You can see below that Lisa is the top-performing Sales person

	A	B	C
3	Sales Person	Product	Sales
4	Lisa		$5,569.76
5		Filing cabinet	$299.94
6		TV cabinet	$299.99
7		Office chair	$559.92
8		Table	$809.91
9		3 seater Sofa	$3,600.00
10	Sally		$4,839.81
11		Desk	$159.98
12		Stool	$199.95
13		Filing cabinet	$199.96
14		Office chair	$279.96
15		TV cabinet	$1,199.96
16		2 seater Sofa	$2,800.00
17	John		$2,119.77
18		Table	$179.98
19		Office chair	$279.96
20		Stool	$359.91
21		Filing cabinet	$399.92
22		3 seater Sofa	$900.00
23	Jim		$1,889.77
24		Office chair	$139.98
25		Coffee table	$299.95
26		Desk	$399.95
27		Filing cabinet	$449.91
28		TV cabinet	$599.98
29	Grand Total		$14,419.11

4) If you want to sort the sales of furniture from highest to lowest for each Sales person, you just select a cell in the Value column. In my example, I select cell C7, for instance. You then just repeat step 2

5) The pivot table is now not only sorted by total sales by Sales person but also by sales of furniture for each Sales person in descending order

	A	B	C
3	Sales Person	Product	Sales
4	Lisa		$5,569.76
5		3 seater Sofa	$3,600.00
6		Table	$809.91
7		Office chair	$559.92
8		TV cabinet	$299.99
9		Filing cabinet	$299.94
10	Sally		$4,839.81
11		2 seater Sofa	$2,800.00
12		TV cabinet	$1,199.96
13		Office chair	$279.96
14		Filing cabinet	$199.96
15		Stool	$199.95
16		Desk	$159.98
17	John		$2,119.77
18		3 seater Sofa	$900.00
19		Filing cabinet	$399.92
20		Stool	$359.91
21		Office chair	$279.96
22		Table	$179.98
23	Jim		$1,889.77
24		TV cabinet	$599.98
25		Filing cabinet	$449.91
26		Desk	$399.95
27		Coffee table	$299.95
28		Office chair	$139.98
29	Grand Total		$14,419.11

Another way to sort is by using the **Sort** command button. Let's say I want to sort the pivot table in alphabetical order of the Sales person's name. Here is how to do this:

1) Select a cell in the column in the pivot table you would like to sort. In this example, I select cell A10

2) From the ribbon, select the **Data** tab and under the **Sort & Filter** group, click the **Sort** command button

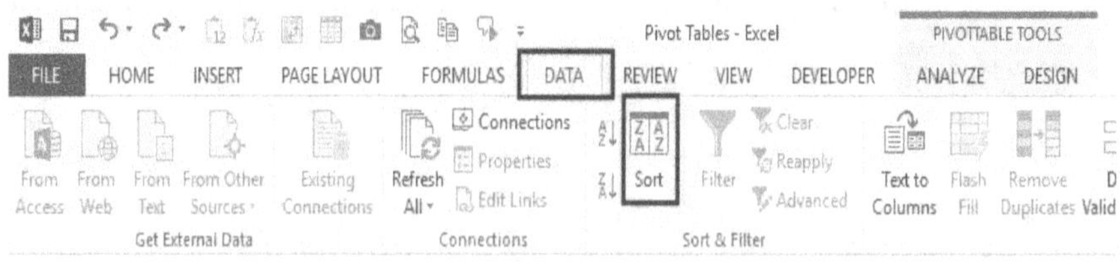

3) In the Sort dialog box, choose whether you want to sort in ascending or descending order, and then from the appropriate field, select the column you want to sort from the drop-down box. In this example, I want to sort in ascending order, and I want to sort by the Sales Person column

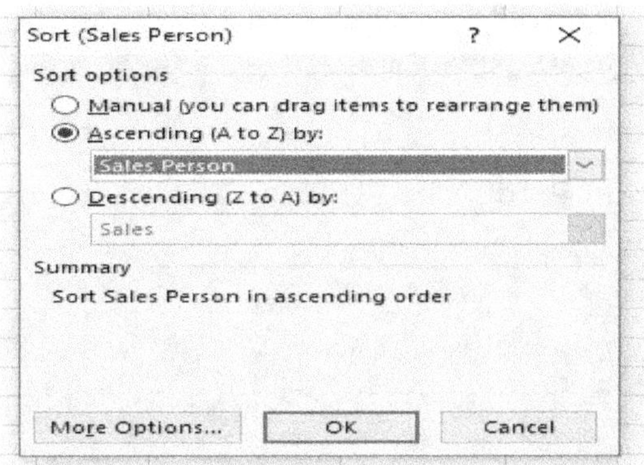

4) The pivot tableis now sorted alphabetically by Sales person name

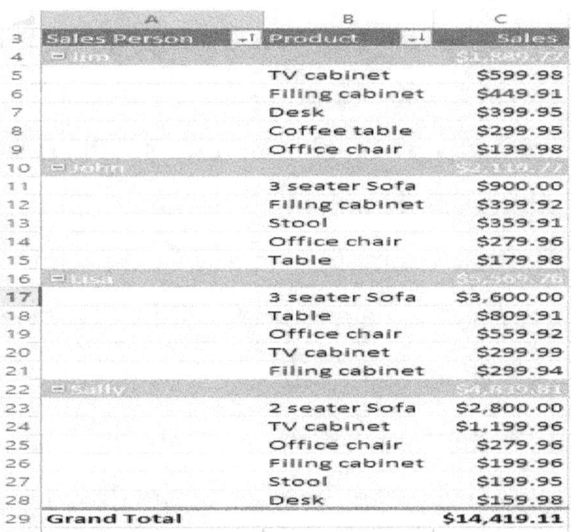

You can follow the same process for the values column, but instead of sorting alphabetically, it will give you the option to sort by value from smallest to largest or largest to smallest.

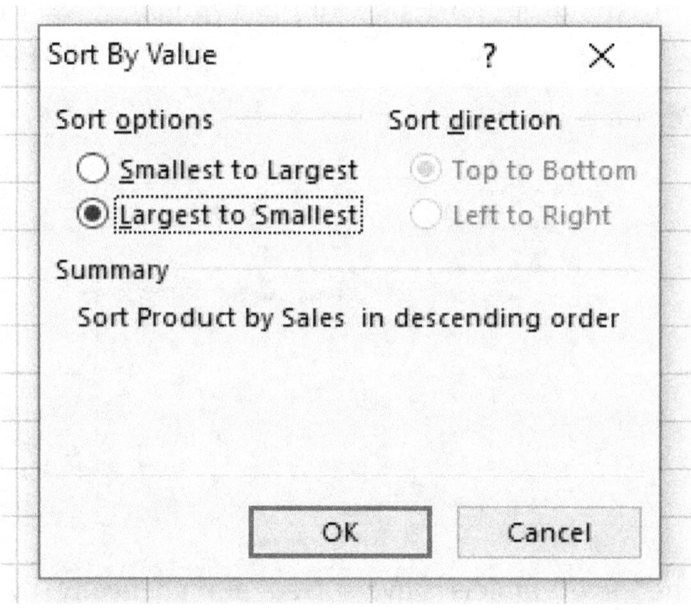

Filtering a Pivot Table

Filtering allows you to view specific information in the pivot table. It works in the same way as filtering data in a worksheet. When you create a pivot table, the filters will already be in the column headings by default. You do not need to apply filters manually. In this example, I want to see the information relating to a 3-seater sofa and filing cabinet. Here are the steps to do this:

1) Click on the filter on the column you want to filter. In this example, I click on the filter in the Product column

	A	B	C
3	Sales Person	Product	Sales
4	⊟ Lisa		$5,569.76
5		3 seater Sofa	$3,600.00
6		Table	$809.91
7		Office chair	$559.92
8		TV cabinet	$299.99
9		Filing cabinet	$299.94
10	⊟ Sally		$4,839.81
11		2 seater Sofa	$2,800.00
12		TV cabinet	$1,199.96
13		Office chair	$279.96
14		Filing cabinet	$199.96
15		Stool	$199.95
16		Desk	$159.98
17	⊟ John		$2,119.77
18		3 seater Sofa	$900.00

2) In the filter, uncheck the boxes against the items you don't want to see and check the boxes against the items you want to see. A quick way to do this is to click the **Select All** check box. This will uncheck all the boxes. You can then check the boxes against the items you want to see. In this example, I check the 3-seater sofa and filing cabinet boxes. Once done, click the **OK** button

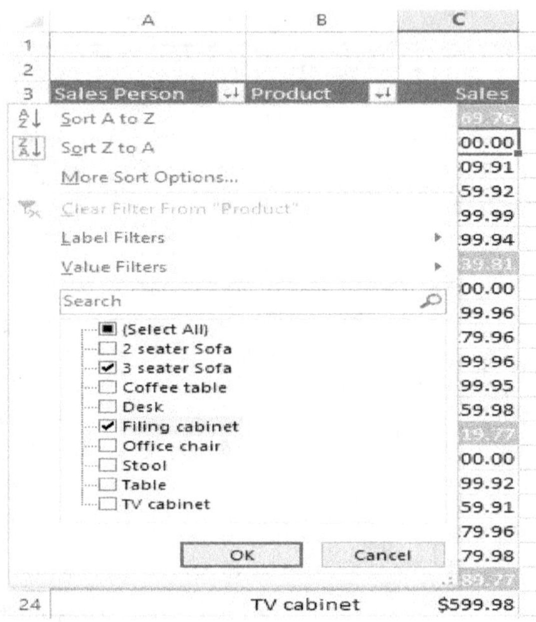

3) The pivot table now just shows the data relating to 3-seater sofas and filing cabinets

Advanced Filtering

You can perform advanced filtering to your pivot table. This provides further flexibility to filtering a pivot table. Let's say I only want to see information for Sales people who have made total sales of over $3,000. Here are the steps on how to do this:

1) Click on a column filter. In this example, I clicked on the Sales Person filter

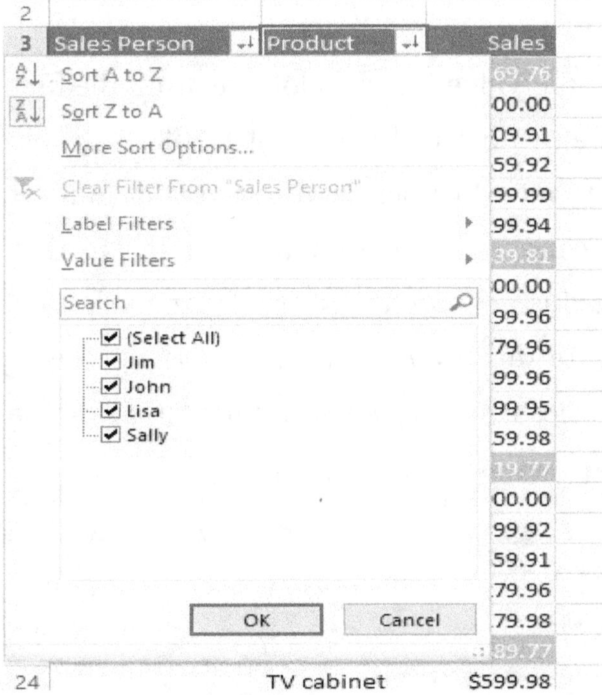

2) Because I want to filter by sales, I select **Value Filters,** and then in the second menu, I select **Greater Than**

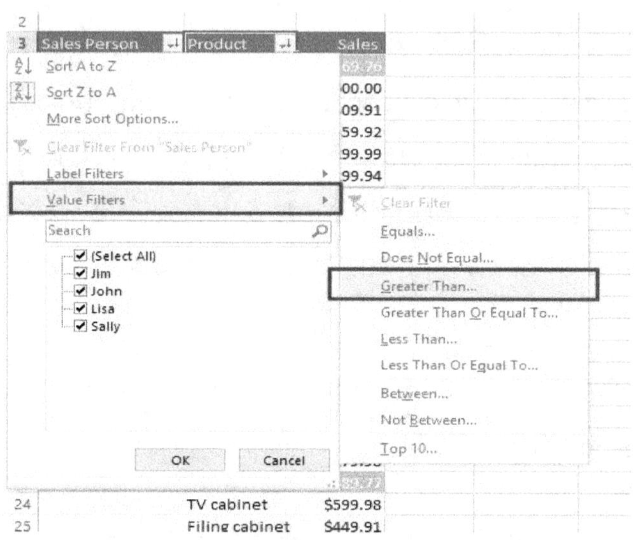

3) In the Value Filter dialog box from the first drop-down box, select the field you want to filter. In this example, I want to filter by sales. In the second drop-down box, select what condition you want to filter by. In this example, I selected **is greater than**. Finally, in the last field, enter the value. In this example, I want to see all Sales people who have sales over $3000, so I enter 3000 in this field. Click the **OK** button

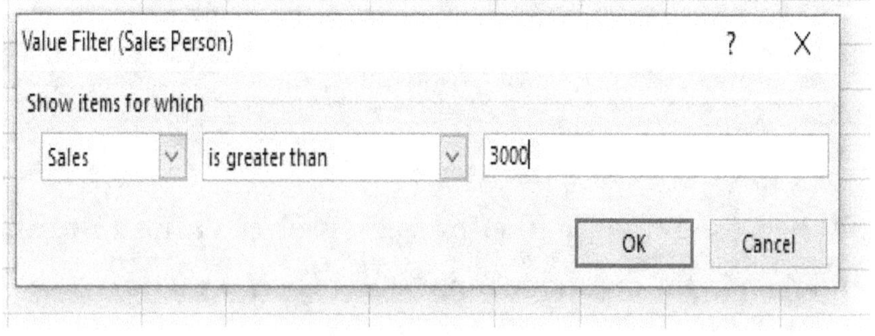

4) The pivot tableis now filtered to show only the Sales people who have sales greater than $3000

	Sales Person	Product	Sales
2			
3	Sales Person	Product	Sales
4	⊟ Lisa		$5,569.76
5		3 seater Sofa	$3,600.00
6		Table	$809.91
7		Office chair	$559.92
8		TV cabinet	$299.99
9		Filing cabinet	$299.94
10	⊟ Sally		$4,839.81
11		2 seater Sofa	$2,800.00
12		TV cabinet	$1,199.96
13		Office chair	$279.96
14		Filing cabinet	$199.96
15		Stool	$199.95
16		Desk	$159.98
17	Grand Total		$10,409.57

Clearing a Filter

If you want to clear any filters applied to your pivot table, then follow these steps:

1) Select any cell in the pivot table

2) In the ribbon, click the **Data** tab, and under the **Sort & Filter** group, click on the **Clear** command button

3) The filters have now all cleared

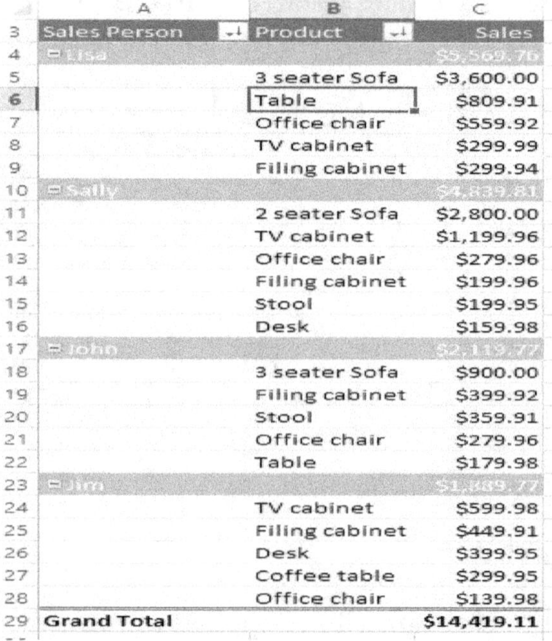

An alternative way to clearing filters is to select the column filter on the column which has been filtered, and from the menu, click **Clear Filter From**

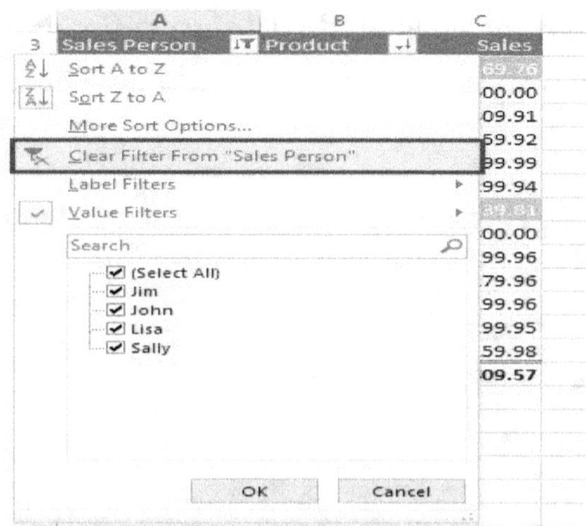

Grouping Pivot Table Items

Grouping is a very useful feature to make your pivot table look more organized. Grouping allows you to group related items together. You can group row and column labels. Now I will give you an example of how to group by date.

In the pivot table below, I have a list of sales by date. The date starts from the 4th August 2019 through to 7th May 2020. I want to summarise the sales by month and year.

Sales Date	Sum of Sales
04/08/2019	$399.95
05/08/2019	$279.96
07/11/2019	$139.98
19/11/2019	$399.92
22/11/2019	$809.91
04/12/2019	$199.96
08/12/2019	$3,600.00
15/12/2019	$449.91
21/12/2019	$179.98
04/01/2020	$2,800.00
09/01/2020	$559.92
19/01/2020	$359.91
04/02/2020	$299.95
08/02/2020	$1,199.96
19/02/2020	$299.94
06/03/2020	$900.00
07/03/2020	$599.98
17/03/2020	$199.95
02/04/2020	$299.99
28/04/2020	$279.96
07/05/2020	$159.98
Grand Total	**$14,419.11**

These are the steps to group by month and year:

1) Right-click any date and select **Group** from the shortcut menu

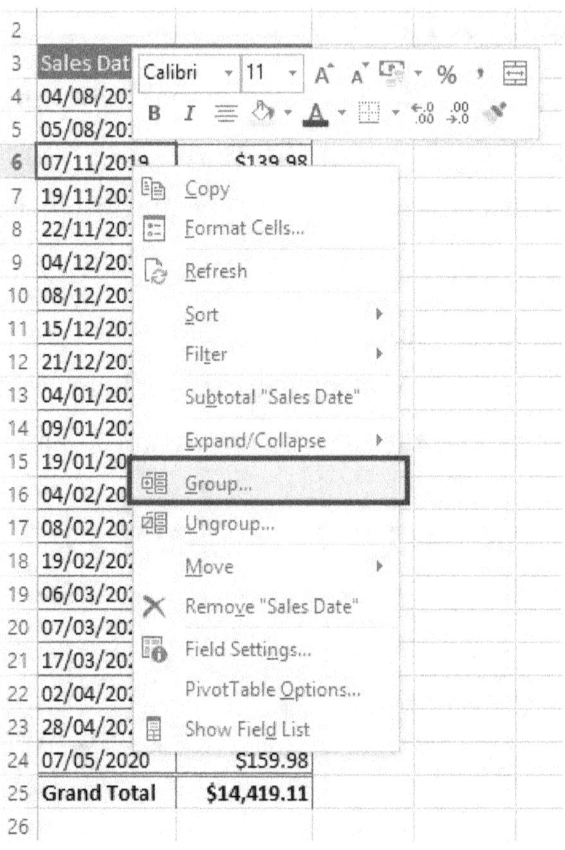

2) In the grouping dialog box, I select **Months** and **Years** as these are the ones I want to group by. Check that the starting and ending dates are correct. Once you are happy, select the **OK** button

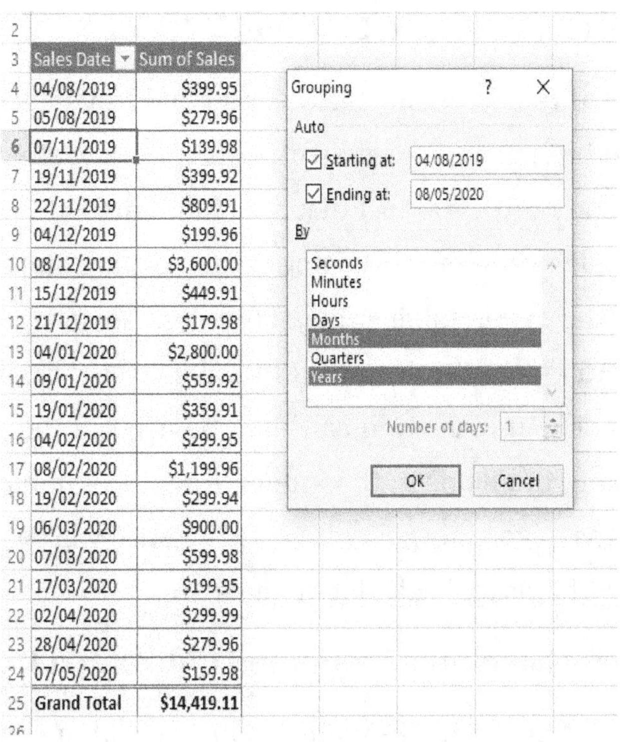

3) The pivot table is now grouped by month and year

Calculated Fields and Calculated Items

You can uutilize custom formulas with pivot tables by using calculated items and calculated fields. These custom formulas are not standard formulas that you can enter into cells. These are formulas you enter in dialog boxes and are stored with the data in the pivot table. The alternative to using calculated fields is to create the formulas in the source data in separate columns. The information can then be used in the pivot table by dragging the fields in the Filters, Rows, Columns, or Values area of the pivot table Fields pane. First, I will explain what calculated fields and calculated items are.

What are Calculated Fields and Calculated Items?

Calculated fields and calculated items can often confuse pivot table users and, as such, are not used as often as they could be. I will explain each one below:

Calculated Field – This is a new field that is created from other fields in the pivot table. The number of other fields will be used in its estimation. A calculated field must be in the Values area of the pivot table Fields pane. You can't use them in the Filters, Rows, or Columns section of the pivot table Fields pane.

Calculated Items – This uses the contents of other items in the field of a pivot table. A calculated item must be in the Filters, Rows, or Columns area of the pivot table Fields pane. You can't use calculated items in the Values area of the pivot table Fields pane.

How to Create a Calculated Field?

To conduct measurements on certain fields in the pivot table, use measured fields. In the pivot table, you can't insert new rows or columns and write formulas in them like you can with a normal worksheet range. To overcome this, you can create a measured field.

Now let's look at an example of how to create a measured field. Below is the pivot table which shows the sales by Sales Person and what month and year they have made the sales along with how many units they have sold. My goal is to work out the average sales per unit for each row. The calculation will be =Sales / Units.

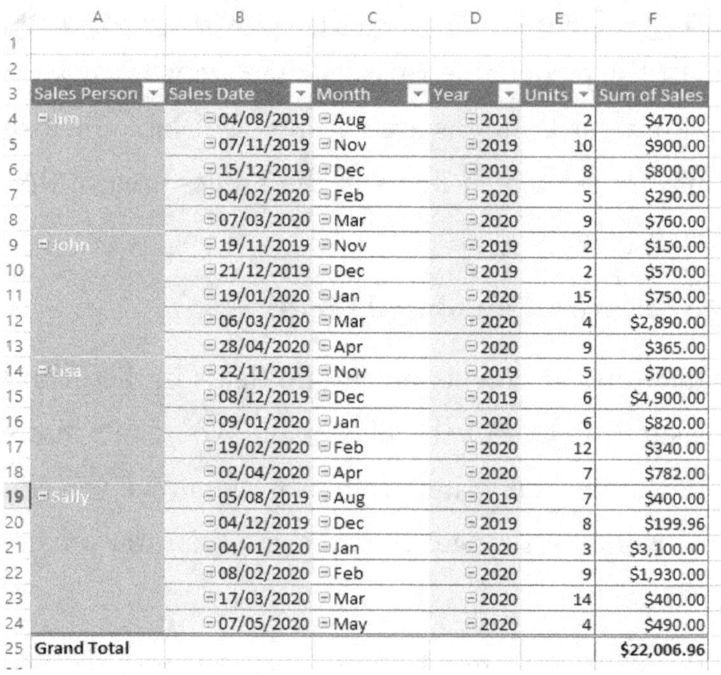

	Sales Person	Sales Date	Month	Year	Units	Sum of Sales
4	☐ Jim	☐ 04/08/2019	☐ Aug	☐ 2019	2	$470.00
5		☐ 07/11/2019	☐ Nov	☐ 2019	10	$900.00
6		☐ 15/12/2019	☐ Dec	☐ 2019	8	$800.00
7		☐ 04/02/2020	☐ Feb	☐ 2020	5	$290.00
8		☐ 07/03/2020	☐ Mar	☐ 2020	9	$760.00
9	☐ John	☐ 19/11/2019	☐ Nov	☐ 2019	2	$150.00
10		☐ 21/12/2019	☐ Dec	☐ 2019	2	$570.00
11		☐ 19/01/2020	☐ Jan	☐ 2020	15	$750.00
12		☐ 06/03/2020	☐ Mar	☐ 2020	4	$2,890.00
13		☐ 28/04/2020	☐ Apr	☐ 2020	9	$365.00
14	☐ Lisa	☐ 22/11/2019	☐ Nov	☐ 2019	5	$700.00
15		☐ 08/12/2019	☐ Dec	☐ 2019	6	$4,900.00
16		☐ 09/01/2020	☐ Jan	☐ 2020	6	$820.00
17		☐ 19/02/2020	☐ Feb	☐ 2020	12	$340.00
18		☐ 02/04/2020	☐ Apr	☐ 2020	7	$782.00
19	☐ Sally	☐ 05/08/2019	☐ Aug	☐ 2019	7	$400.00
20		☐ 04/12/2019	☐ Dec	☐ 2019	8	$199.96
21		☐ 04/01/2020	☐ Jan	☐ 2020	3	$3,100.00
22		☐ 08/02/2020	☐ Feb	☐ 2020	9	$1,930.00
23		☐ 17/03/2020	☐ Mar	☐ 2020	14	$400.00
24		☐ 07/05/2020	☐ May	☐ 2020	4	$490.00
25	Grand Total					$22,006.96

Here are the steps to create the calculated area:

1) Click any cell in the pivot table

2) In the ribbon, click a **Analyze** tab, and under the **Calculations,** field select **Calculated Field**

3) In a Name text box of the Insert Calculated Field dialogue, type a field name such as Profit. In this

example, I have called it 'Average Sales per Unit. In a **Formula** field, you have to create the formula. The formula for the average sales per unit is =Sales / Units. I first select the 'Sales' field under the **Fields** section and then click the **Insert Field** button. I want to use the division operator, so I enter a '/' after the Sales field. I then select the 'Units' field and click the **Insert Field** button

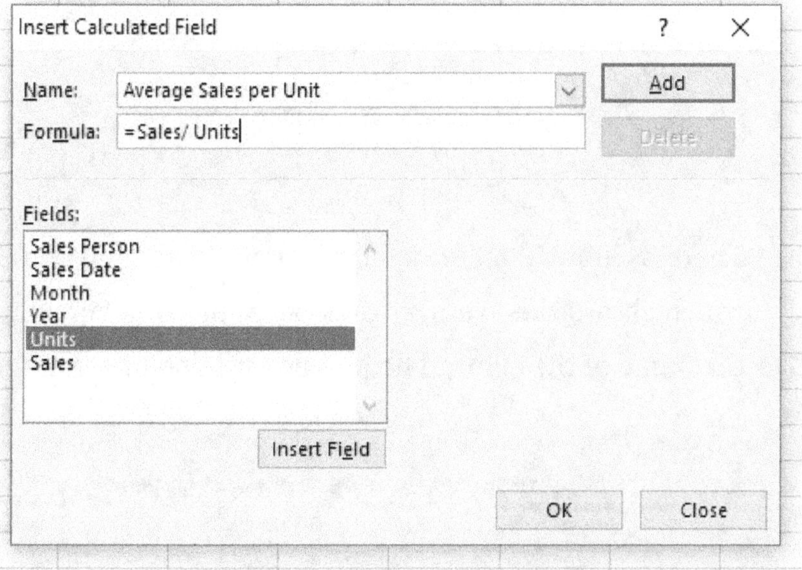

4) Once the formula has been entered, press the **Add** button and then **OK**

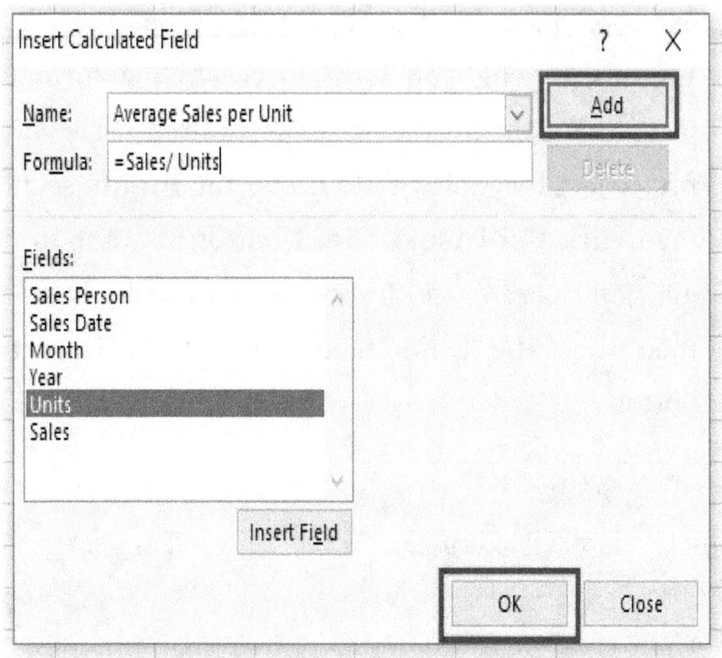

5) There is now a column at the end of the pivot table which shows the average sales per unit. You can change the name of the column header as explained in chapter 4

	Sales Person	Sales Date	Month	Year	Units	Sum of Sales	Sum of Average Sales per Unit
1							
2							
3	Sales Person	Sales Date	Month	Year	Units	Sum of Sales	Sum of Average Sales per Unit
4	Jim	04/08/2019	Aug	2019	2	$470.00	$235.00
5		07/11/2019	Nov	2019	10	$900.00	$90.00
6		15/12/2019	Dec	2019	8	$800.00	$100.00
7		04/02/2020	Feb	2020	5	$290.00	$58.00
8		07/03/2020	Mar	2020	9	$760.00	$84.44
9	John	19/11/2019	Nov	2019	2	$150.00	$75.00
10		21/12/2019	Dec	2019	2	$570.00	$285.00
11		19/01/2020	Jan	2020	15	$750.00	$50.00
12		06/03/2020	Mar	2020	4	$2,890.00	$722.50
13		28/04/2020	Apr	2020	9	$365.00	$40.56
14	Luke	22/11/2019	Nov	2019	5	$700.00	$140.00
15		08/12/2019	Dec	2019	6	$4,900.00	$816.67
16		09/01/2020	Jan	2020	6	$820.00	$136.67
17		19/02/2020	Feb	2020	12	$340.00	$28.33
18		02/04/2020	Apr	2020	7	$782.00	$111.71
19	Sally	05/08/2019	Aug	2019	7	$400.00	$57.14
20		04/12/2019	Dec	2019	8	$199.96	$25.00
21		04/01/2020	Jan	2020	3	$3,100.00	$1,033.33
22		08/02/2020	Feb	2020	9	$1,930.00	$214.44
23		17/03/2020	Mar	2020	14	$400.00	$28.57
24		07/05/2020	May	2020	4	$490.00	$122.50
25	Grand Total					$22,006.96	$149.71

How to Create a Calculated Item?

You can also use measure items to perform calculations in the pivot table. This is equivalent to adding new rows to the data source, i.e., rows which contain formulas that refer to other rows.

Now I will show you how to create a calculated item. Below is the pivot table that shows the sales by year for each Salesperson. In this example, I want to create two calculated items that show how much bonus each salesperson will receive in 2019 and 2020. The bonus applied for each year are as follows:

2019 – 15% of 2019 sales

2020 – 20% of 2020 sales

	A	B	C
1			
2			
3	Sales Person ▼	Year ▼	Sum of Sales
4	⊟ Jim	2019	$2,170.00
5		2020	$1,050.00
6	⊟ John	2019	$720.00
7		2020	$4,005.00
8	⊟ Lisa	2019	$5,600.00
9		2020	$1,942.00
10	⊟ Sally	2019	$599.96
11		2020	$5,920.00
12	Grand Total		$22,006.96
13			

Here are the methods to make the calculated items:

1) Select a cell in a Row or Column area of a pivot table. In this example, I select a cell in a Year column

2) In the ribbon, click a **Analyze** tab, and under the **Calculations,** group select **Calculated Item**

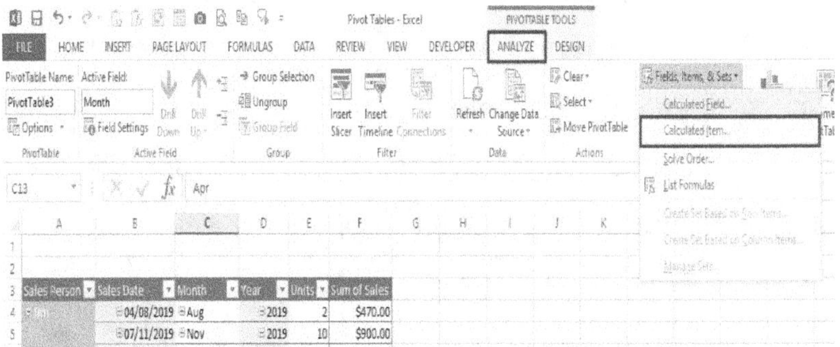

3) In the Insert Calculated Item in the dialog box, enter a name in the **Name** field. In this example, I entered '2019 Bonus'. In the **Formula,** the field enters the desired formula. I want to show a bonus of 15% for all sales in 2019, so I entered the formula =15%* '2019'. To insert the year 2019 in the formula, I clicked on the 'Year' field under **Fields** and then selected '2019' under **Items,** and then clicked the **Insert Item** button

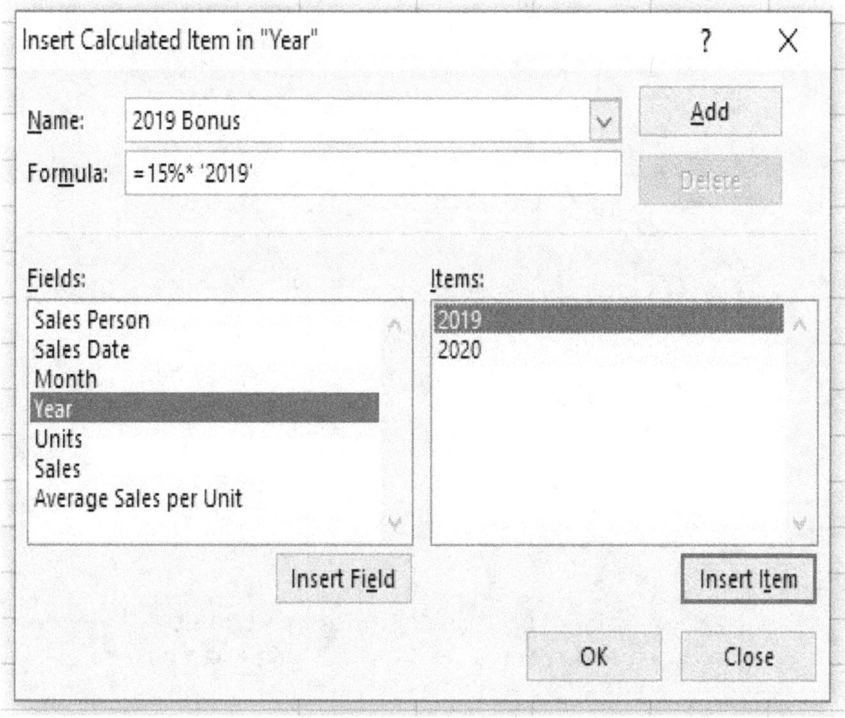

4) Click on the **Add** button and then the **OK** button

5) Repeat steps 1 to 4 to create the bonus for 2020

6) The 2019 and 2020 bonus will now appear for each Salesperson

	Sales Person	Year	Sum of Sales
2			
3	Sales Person ▼	Year ▼	Sum of Sales
4	⊟ Jim	2019	$2,170.00
5		2020	$1,050.00
6		2019 Bonus	$325.50
7		2020 Bonus	$210.00
8	⊟ John	2019	$720.00
9		2020	$4,005.00
10		2019 Bonus	$108.00
11		2020 Bonus	$801.00
12	⊟ Lisa	2019	$5,600.00
13		2020	$1,942.00
14		2019 Bonus	$840.00
15		2020 Bonus	$388.40
16	⊟ Sally	2019	$599.96
17		2020	$5,920.00
18		2019 Bonus	$89.99
19		2020 Bonus	$1,184.00
20	**Grand Total**		**$25,953.85**
21			

Referencing Cells in the pivot table

You can create formulas outside the pivot table by simply clicking a cell or a range of cells in the pivot table. You might expect a cell reference such as C5 but what Excel will actually return is the GETPIVOTDATA function.

What is the GETPIVOTDATA Function?

The GETPIVOTDATA function is designed to extract data from a pivot table. It is used to ensure that formulas will reference the desired cells even if the pivot table has changed format.

Let's look at an example. In the previous chapter, I explained how to create a calculated field that shows the average sales per unit. Now I want to replicate this formula outside the pivot table in cell E4. I used the point and click method. When I selected cell C4, Excel returned:

=GETPIVOTDATA ("Sales", $A$3,"Sales Person","Jim","Units",2)

I then entered the division operator and then clicked on cell B4. Notice the second part of the formula refers to the actual cell, i.e., B4. This is because the Units field is in the Rows area of the pivot table and not the Values area. I then just copied the formula down to cell E22.

| | E4 | | | f_x | =GETPIVOTDATA("Sales",$A$3,"Sales Person","Jim","Units",2)/B4 |

	A	B	C	D	E	F	G	H	I
2									
3	Sales Per	Units	Sum of Sales		Average sales per unit				
4	⊟Jim	2	$470.00		$235.00				
5		5	$290.00		$94.00				
6		8	$800.00		$58.75				
7		9	$760.00		$52.22				
8		10	$900.00		$47.00				
9	⊟John	2	$720.00		$235.00				
10		4	$2,890.00		$117.50				
11		9	$365.00		$52.22				
12		15	$750.00		$31.33				
13	⊟Lisa	5	$700.00		$94.00				
14		6	$5,720.00		$78.33				
15		7	$782.00		$67.14				
16		12	$340.00		$39.17				
17	⊟Sally	3	$3,100.00		$156.67				
18		4	$490.00		$117.50				
19		7	$400.00		$67.14				
20		8	$199.96		$58.75				
21		9	$1,930.00		$52.22				
22		14	$400.00		$33.57				
23	Grand Total		$22,006.96						
24									

Note: The GETPIVOTDATA function can only retrieve data that is visible in the pivot table; otherwise, it will return an error.

You can manually type the cell references in if you do not want to see the GETPIVOTDATA function in your formulas. In the below example, I typed in the formula = C4/B4 in cell E4 and then copied the formula down to cell E22.

E4		f_x	=C4/B4	

	A	B	C	D	E
1					
2					
3	Sales Pers ▼	Units ▼	Sum of Sales		Average sales per unit
4	⊟ Jim	2	$470.00		$235.00
5		5	$290.00		$58.00
6		8	$800.00		$100.00
7		9	$760.00		$84.44
8		10	$900.00		$90.00
9	⊟ John	2	$720.00		$360.00
10		4	$2,890.00		$722.50
11		9	$365.00		$40.56
12		15	$750.00		$50.00
13	⊟ Lisa	5	$700.00		$140.00
14		6	$5,720.00		$953.33
15		7	$782.00		$111.71
16		12	$340.00		$28.33
17	⊟ Sally	3	$3,100.00		$1,033.33
18		4	$490.00		$122.50
19		7	$400.00		$57.14
20		8	$199.96		$25.00
21		9	$1,930.00		$214.44
22		14	$400.00		$28.57
23	Grand Total		$22,006.96		

Turning off the GETPIVOTDATA Function

If you prefer, you can turn off the GETPIVOTDATA function if you would rather have Excel use cell references instead.

To turn the setting off, click on the **Analyze** tab in the ribbon, and under the **PivotTable** group, click on the drop-down arrow from the **Options** command button. Finally, click on **Generate GetPivotData**.

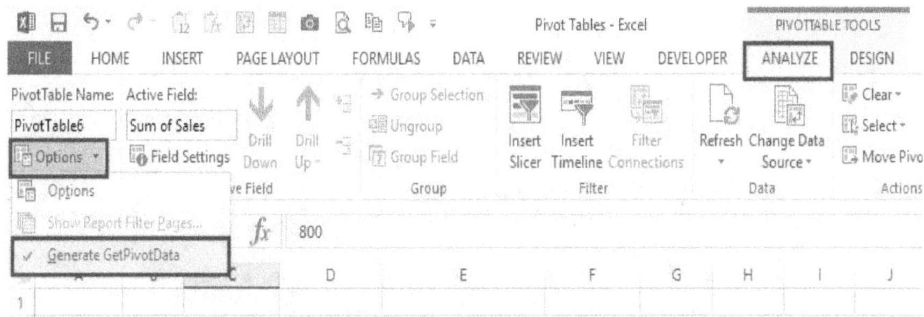

Creating Pivot Charts

A pivot chart is similar to a normal chart in Excel. It visualizes the data in the pivot tableso users can interpret and analyze the information more easily. Pivot charts and pivot tables are connected with each other. A pivot chart comes into its own if there is a lot of information in the pivot table, as you can see the trends in a snapshot. The great thing about pivot charts is that you can easily chop and change the information in the pivot table, and the pivot chart will change accordingly. For example, you can move a field from the Rows area to the Columns area in the pivot table Fields pane, and the pivot chart will change accordingly.

How to Create a Pivot Chart?

I will now show you the steps on how to create a pivot chart. I will use the pivot table below, which shows the sales of each furniture item made by a Sales person to create a column chart. The Sales Person and the Product fields are in the Rows area of the pivot table Fields pane, and the Sales is in the Values area of the pivot table Fields pane.

	A	B	C
1			
2			
3	Sales Person	Product	Sales
4	⊟ Jim	Coffee table	$299.95
5		Desk	$399.95
6		Filing cabinet	$449.91
7		Office chair	$139.98
8		TV cabinet	$599.98
9	⊟ John	3 seater Sofa	$900.00
10		Filing cabinet	$399.92
11		Office chair	$279.96
12		Stool	$359.91
13		Table	$179.98
14	⊟ Lisa	3 seater Sofa	$3,600.00
15		Filing cabinet	$299.94
16		Office chair	$559.92
17		Table	$809.91
18		TV cabinet	$299.99
19	⊟ Sally	2 seater Sofa	$2,800.00
20		Desk	$159.98
21		Filing cabinet	$199.96
22		Office chair	$279.96
23		Stool	$199.95
24		TV cabinet	$1,199.96
25	Grand Total		$14,419.11
26			

1) Click any cell in the pivot table

2) In the ribbon, click on the **Insert** tab, and from the **Charts** group, select from the range of charts that are available. In this example, I will choose the **Column Chart**

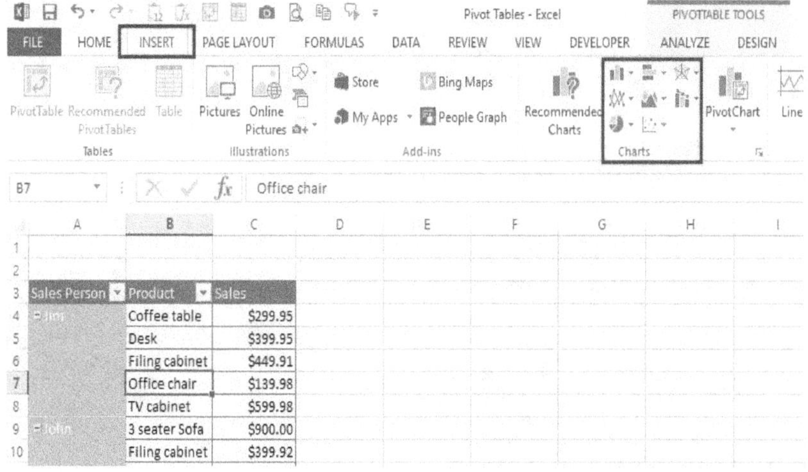

Note: You can also select a chart from **Recommended Charts** or the **PivotChart** command buttons. If you press the **Recommended Charts** command button, then Excel will recommend the best chart to use based on the structure and data of a pivot table

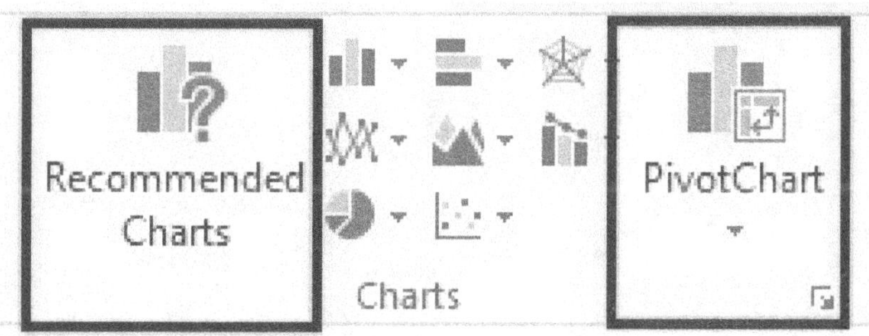

3) The pivot chart is now created

Sales Person	Product	Sales
⊟ Jim	Coffee table	$299.95
	Desk	$399.95
	Filing cabinet	$449.91
	Office chair	$139.98
	TV cabinet	$599.98
⊟ John	3 seater Sofa	$900.00
	Filing cabinet	$399.92
	Office chair	$279.96
	Stool	$359.91
	Table	$179.98
⊟ Lisa	3 seater Sofa	$3,600.00
	Filing cabinet	$299.94
	Office chair	$559.92
	Table	$809.91
	TV cabinet	$299.99
⊟ Sally	2 seater Sofa	$2,800.00
	Desk	$159.98

Resizing the Pivot Chart

You can resize the pivot chart by clicking the chart to make it active and then using the handles on each side to make it smaller or larger. If you click and drag the top or bottom handles, then it will make the chart taller or smaller. If you click and drag the left or right side, then it will make it narrower or wider.

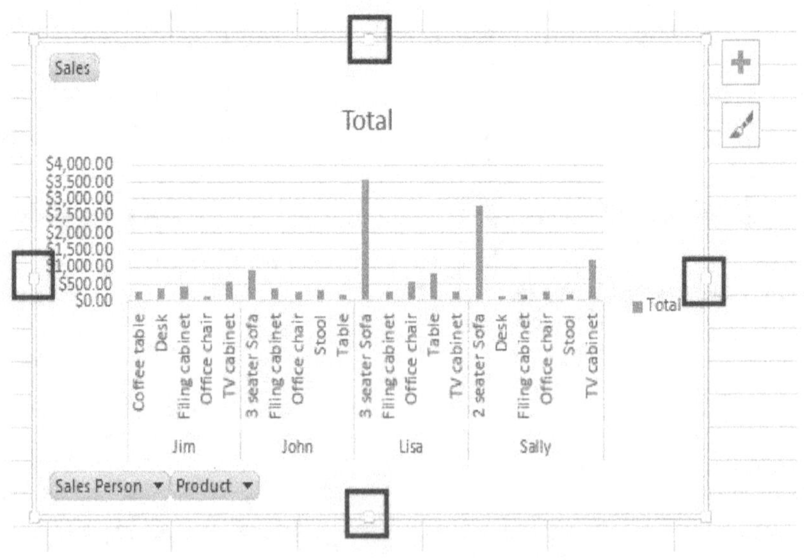

Formatting the Pivot Chart

Like with formatting an Excel chart, you can also format a pivot chart in the same way. You first click on the chart to make it active and then click on the **Chart Elements** button, which is located at the top right of the chart. You can then change various elements of the chart, such as changing the chart title, changing the Legend name and position, whether to include axis titles, and so on.

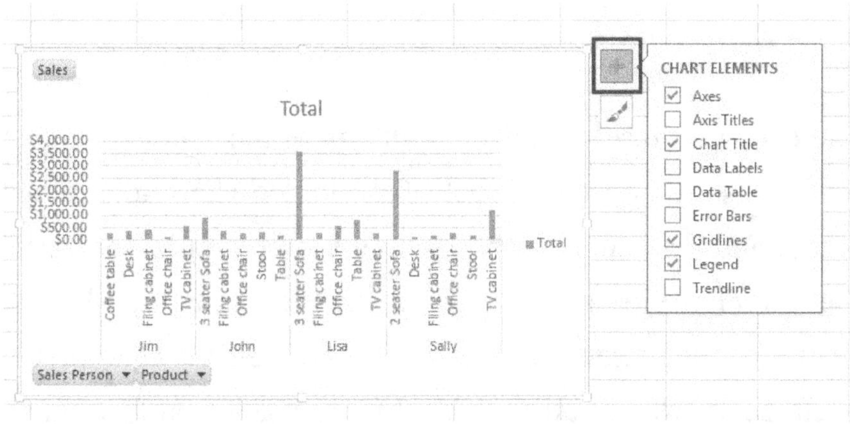

In this example, I have renamed the chart title 'Sales by Sales Person. I have also included axis titles on the x and y-axis and named them, and also taken out the Legend.

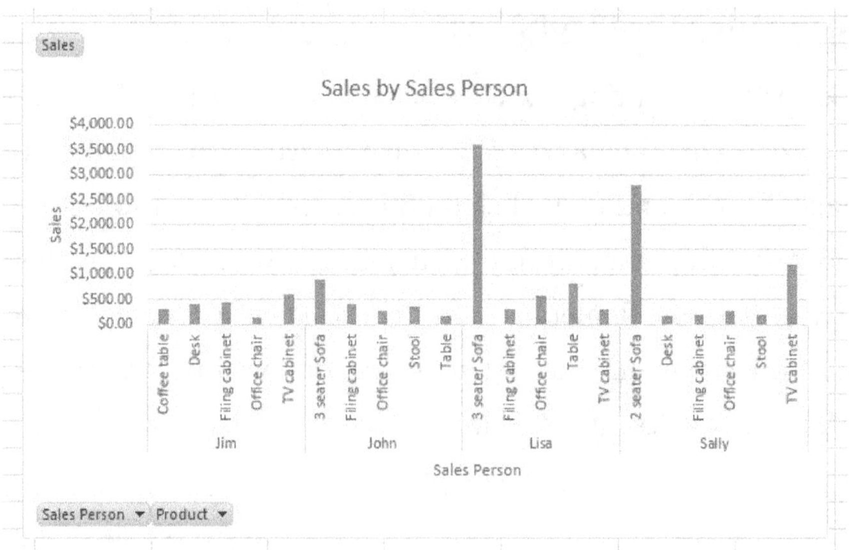

You can also quickly change the design of the chart to make it more visually attractive. Just click on the chart to make it active, and then click on the **Design** tab in the ribbon. Under the **Chart Styles** group, click on the down arrow, which is located at the bottom right, to see all the available chart styles. Each chart style contains different fonts, colours, and designs.

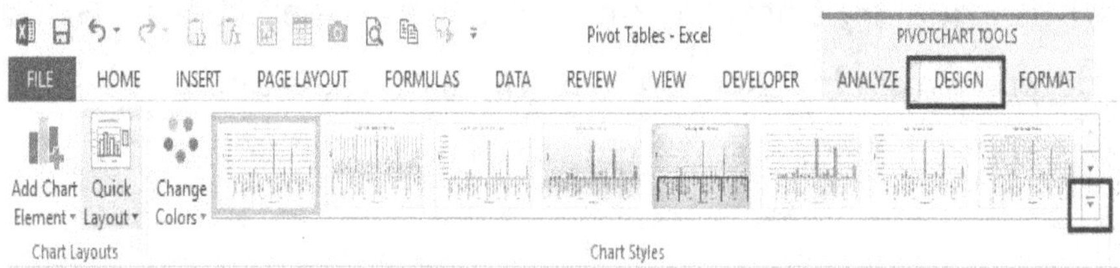

In my example, I have chosen Style 3.

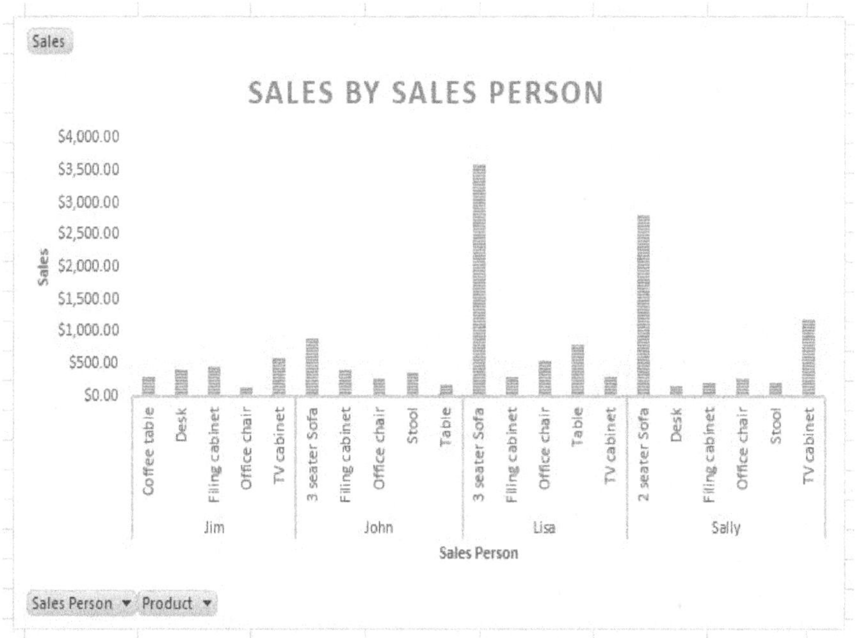

Changing Chart Type

If you decide you want a different chart instead, then you can change the chart type. To do this, click on the **Design** tab in the ribbon, and under the **Type** group, click the **Change Chart Type** command button.

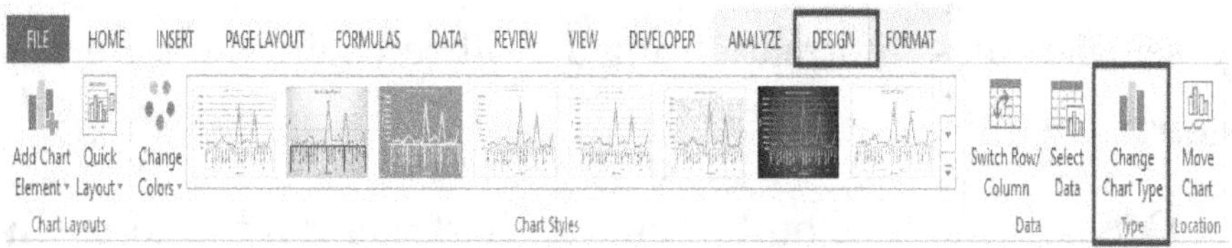

You can then choose from the list of available charts. Once you have chosen a chart, click the **OK** button.

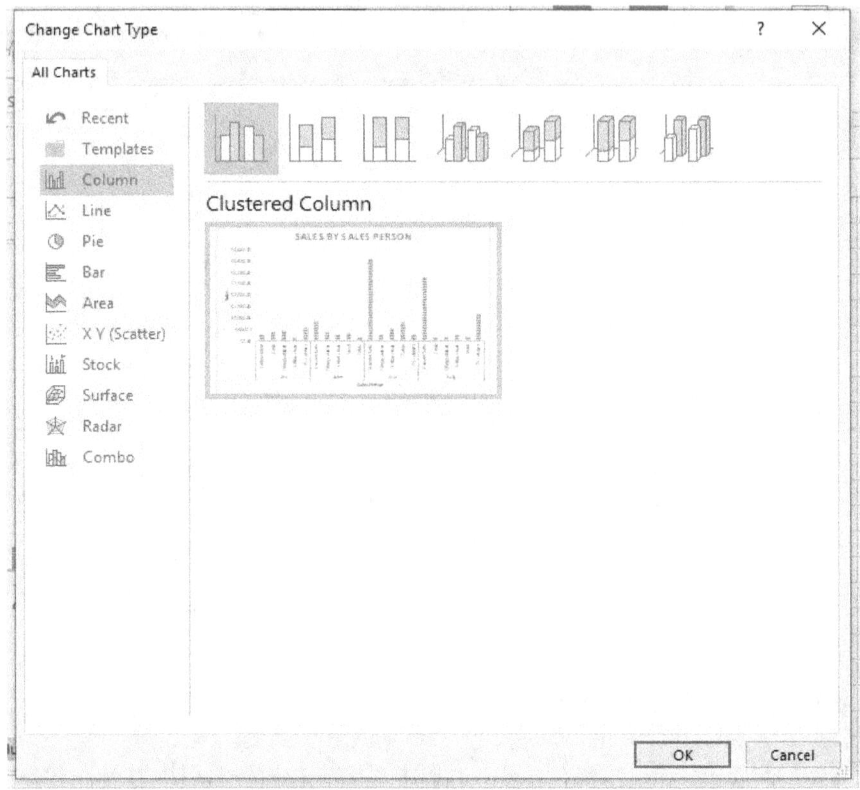

Filtering Pivot Charts

You can filter a pivot chart, so it only displays the information you want to see, and it will hide the rest. Let's say I only want to see the sales information for the office chair. Here are the steps to do this:

1) Select the field button on the chart you want to filter. In this example, I want to filter the Product field as I only want to see the sales information for the office chair

2) Check the box or boxes against the items you want to see and uncheck the boxes against the items you don't want to see. In this example, I have checked the office chair box and unchecked the other checkboxes

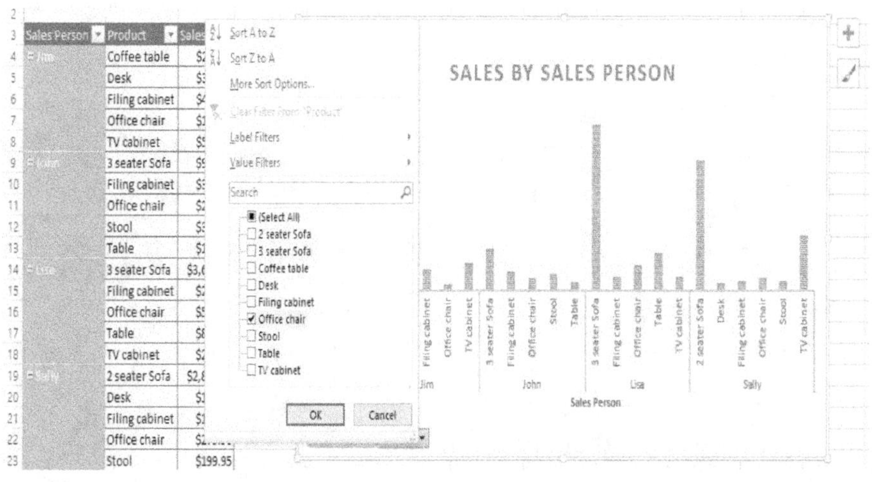

3) You can now only see the sales information for the office chair in the pivot chart. Notice that the pivot tablehas also been filtered

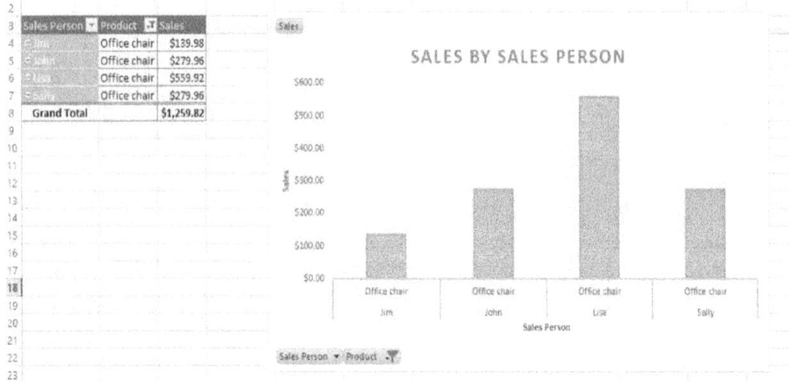

4) To clear the filter, click the field button that was filtered in the pivot chart, and then from the menu, select **Clear Filter From**

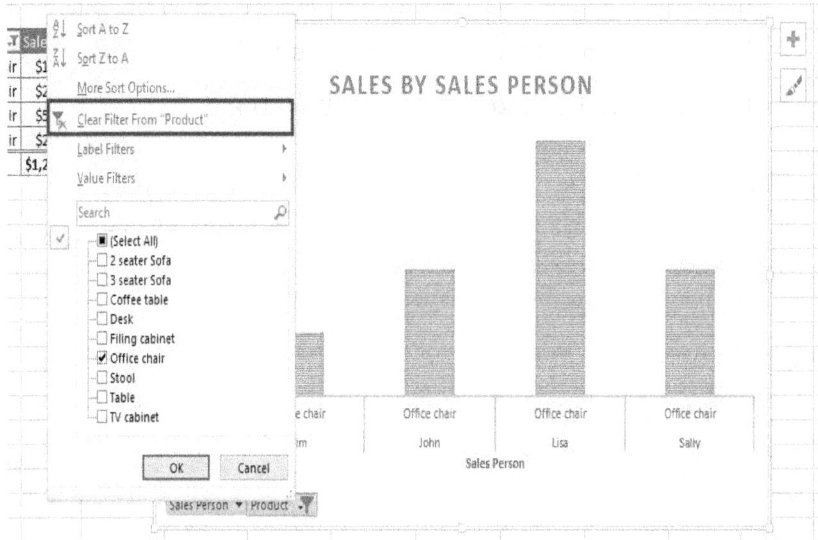

5) The pivot chart is now un-filtered

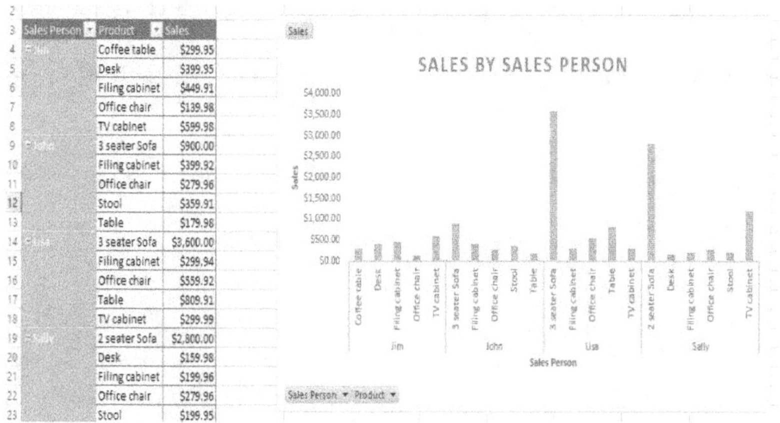

Sales Person	Product	Sales
Jim	Coffee table	$299.95
	Desk	$399.95
	Filing cabinet	$449.91
	Office chair	$139.98
	TV cabinet	$599.98
John	3 seater Sofa	$900.00
	Filing cabinet	$399.92
	Office chair	$279.96
	Stool	$359.91
	Table	$179.98
Lisa	3 seater Sofa	$3,600.00
	Filing cabinet	$299.94
	Office chair	$559.92
	Table	$809.91
	TV cabinet	$299.99
Sally	2 seater Sofa	$2,800.00
	Desk	$159.98
	Filing cabinet	$199.96
	Office chair	$279.96
	Stool	$199.95

Changing the Structure of the Pivot Chart

You can easily change the pivot chart to show information in a different way. In the previous sections, I created a pivot chart where the Sales Person and Product fields were in the Rows area of the pivot table Fields pane, as shown below.

Let's see what happens if I move the Product field from the Rows area to the Columns area of the pivot table Fields pane like this:

The pivot chart changes. The furniture items now become the legend.

Sales
SALES BY SALES PERSON
$4,000.00
$3,500.00
$3,000.00
$2,500.00
$2,000.00
$1,500.00
$1,000.00
$500.00
$0.00
Sales
Jim
John
Lisa
Sally
Sales Person
Product
2 seater Sofa
3 seater Sofa
Coffee table
Desk
Filing cabinet
Office chair
Stool
Table
TV cabinet
Sales Person

Chapter 5: Formulas and Functions

Formulas, to put it mildly, are the very "bread and butter" of the worksheet. Without formulas, the electronic spreadsheet would be a little better than its green-sheet paper equivalent. Fortunately, Excel gives you the ability to do all your calculations right within the cells of the worksheet without any need for a separate calculator.

The formulas that you build in a spreadsheet can run the gamut from very simple to extremely complex. Formulas can rely totally upon the use of simple operators or the use of built-in functions, both of which describe the type of operation or calculation to perform and the order in which to perform it. Or they can blend the use of operators and functions together. When you use Excel functions in your formulas, you need to understand the particular type of information that a particular function uses in performing its calculations. The information that you supply a function and that it uses in its computation is referred to as the argument(s) of the function.

Formulas 101

From the simple addition formula to the most complex ANOVA statistical variation, all formulas in Microsoft Excel have one thing in common: They all begin with the equal sign (=). This doesn't mean that you always have to type in the equal sign — although if you do, Excel expects that a formula of some type is to follow. When building a formula that uses a built-in function,

oftentimes, you use the Insert Function button on a Formula bar to select and insert the function, in which case, Excel adds the equal opening sign for you.

If you're an old Lotus 1-2-3 user and you still want to type the @ symbol to start a function, Excel accepts the at symbol and automatically converts it into an equal sign the moment that you complete the formula entry. It does mean, however, that each and every completed formula that appears on the Formula bar starts with the equal sign.

When building your formulas, you can use constants that actually contain the number that you want to be used in the calculation (such as "4.5%," "$25.00," or "−78.35"), or you can use cell addresses between the operators or as the arguments of functions. When you create a formula that uses cell addresses, Excel then uses the values that you've input in those cells in calculating the formula. Unlike when using constants in formulas, when you use cell addresses, Excel automatically updates the results calculated by a formula whenever you edit the values in the cells to which it refers.

Formula building methods

You may either write in the cell attributes or point to them in the worksheet while manually creating formulas. When supplying cell addresses for formulas, using the Pointing approach is much simpler and often a lot more foolproof method; when typing in a cell address, you're less likely to find

that you've only designated the incorrect cell than when referring directly to it. As a result, when creating new formulas, stick to pointing instead of typing cell addresses, unless you have to change cell addresses in an equation, and referring to it is either not possible or too much hassle.

Formulas and formatting

When defining a formula that uses operators or functions, Excel picks up the number formatting of the cells that are referenced in the formula. For example, if you add cell A2 to B3, as in =A2+B3 and cell B3 is formatted with the Currency Style format, the result will inherit this format and be displayed in its cell using the Currency Style.

When you use the Pointing method to build a simple formula that defines a sequence of operations, you stop and click the cell or drag through the cell range after typing each operator in the formula. When using the method to build a formula that uses a built-in function, you click the cell or drag through the cell range that you want to be used when defining the function's arguments in the Function Arguments dialog box.

As with the other types of cell entries, you must take some action to complete the formula and enter it into the current cell (such as clicking the Enter button on the Formula bar, pressing the Enter key, or pressing an arrow key). Unlike when entering numeric or text entries, however, you will want to stay clear of clicking another cell to complete the data entry. This is because

when you click a cell when building or editing a formula on the Formula bar, more often than not, you end up not only selecting the new cell but also adding its address to the otherwise complete formula.

When you finish entering a calculation, Excel determines the answer, which is then shown within the worksheet cell. (However, the components of the formula remain clear on the Formula bar while the cell is active.) If you create a formula mistake that prohibits Excel from calculating the equation at all, Excel shows an Alert dialogue box with instructions about how to correct the issue. If you create a mistake that stops Excel from calculating the formula and displaying a correct outcome, the software shows an estimation Error value instead of the intended calculated value.

Editing formulas

As with numeric and text entries, you can edit the contents of formulas either in their cells or on the Formula bar. To edit a formula in its cell, double-click the cell or press F2 to position the insertion pointer in that cell. (Double-clicking the cell positions the insertion pointer in the middle of the formula, whereas pressing F2 positions it at the end of the formula — you can also double-click at the beginning or end of the cell to position the insertion pointer there.) To edit a formula on the Formula bar, use the I-beam mouse to position the insertion point at the place in the formula that needs editing first.

Using excel like a handheld calculator

Sometimes, you may need to actually calculate the number that you need to input in a cell as a constant. Instead of reaching for your pocket calculator to compute the needed value and then manually entering it into a cell of your spreadsheet, you can set up a formula in the cell that returns the number that you need to input and then convert the formula into a constant value. You convert the formula into a constant by pressing F2 to edit the cell, immediately pressing F9 to recalculate the formula and display the result on the Formula bar, and then selecting the Enter button on the Formula bar or pressing the Enter key to input the calculated result into the cell (as though you had manually input the result in the cell).

As soon as you put the Excel program into Edit mode, Excel displays each of the cell references in the formula within the cell in a different color and uses this color to outline the cell or cell range in the worksheet itself. This coloration enables you to quickly identify the cells and their values that are referred to in your formula and, if necessary, modify them as well. You can use any of the four sizing handles that appear around the cell or cell range to modify the cell selection in the worksheet and consequently update the cell references in the formula.

When you AutoSum numbers in a spreadsheet

The easiest and often the most used formula that you will create is the one that totals rows and columns of numbers in your

spreadsheet. Usually, to total a row or column of numbers, you can click the Sum command button (the one with the Σ on it) in the Editing group of the Home tab of the Ribbon. When you click this button, Excel inserts the built-in SUM function into the active cell and simultaneously selects what the program thinks is the most likely range of numbers that you want to be summed.

Instead of taking the time to click the Sum button on the Home tab, it's often faster and easier to simply press Alt+= (equal sign) to insert the SUM function in the current cell and have Excel select the range of cells most likely to be totaled.

Figure 1-1 demonstrates how this works. For this figure, I positioned the cell cursor in cell B7, which is the first cell where I need to build a formula that totals the various parts produced in April. I then clicked the Sum button on the Home tab of the Ribbon.

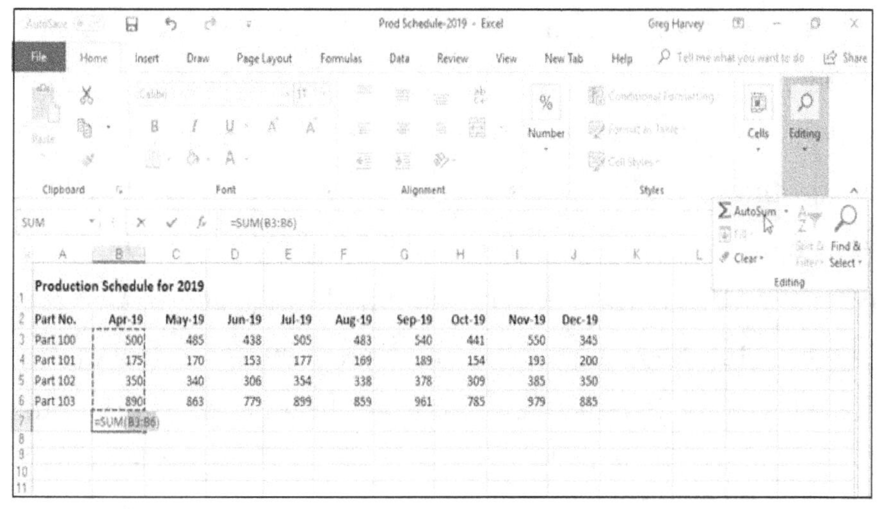

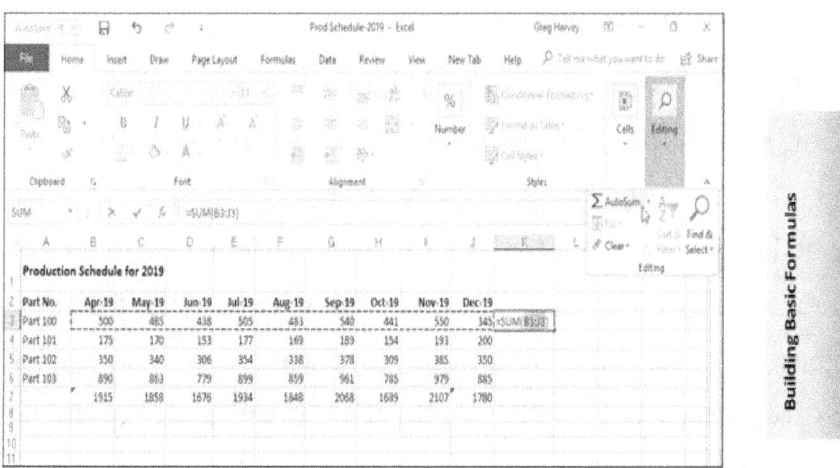

As Figure 1 shows, Excel then inserted an equal sign followed by the SUM function and correctly suggested the cell range B3:B6 as the argument to this function (that is, the range to be summed). Because Excel correctly selected the range to be summed (leaving out the date value in cell B2), all I have to do is click the Enter button on the Formula bar to have the April total calculated.

Figure -2 shows another example of AutoSum to instantly build a SUM formula, this time to total the monthly production numbers for Part 100 in cell K3. Again, all I did to create the formula shown in Figure 1-2 was to select cell K3 and then click the Sum button on the Home tab. Again, Excel correctly selected B3:J3 as the summed range and passed this range to the SUM feature as the statement. To calculate the daily totals for Part 100, all that is left to do is press the Enter button on the Formula bar.

When auto sum doesn't sum

Although the Sum button's primary function is to build formulas with the SUM function that totals ranges of numbers, that's not its only function (pun intended). Indeed, you can have the AutoSum feature build formulas that compute the average value, count the number of values, or return the highest or lowest value in a range — all you have to do is click the drop-down button that's attached to the Sum command button on the Home tab and then click Average, Count Numbers, Max, or Min from its drop-down menu.

Also, don't forget about the Average, Count, and Sum indicator on the Status bar. This indicator automatically shows you the average value, the count of the numbers, and the total of all numbers in the current cell selection. You can use this feature to preview the total that's to be returned by the SUM formula that you create with the AutoSum button by selecting the cell range that contains the numbers to be summed.

If for some reason, AutoSum doesn't select the entire or correct range that you want summed, you can adjust the range by dragging the cell cursor through the cell range or by clicking the marquee around the cell range, which turns the marching ants into a solid colored outline. Then position the mouse pointer on one of the sizing handles at the four corners. When it turns into

a thick white arrowhead pointing to the center of a pair of black double-crossed arrows, drag the outline until it includes all the cells you want to be included in the total.

Keep in mind that all Excel functions enclose their argument(s) in a closed pair of parentheses, as shown in the examples with the SUM function. Even those rare functions that don't require any arguments at all still require the use of a closed pair of parentheses (even when you don't put anything inside of them).

Totals and sums with a Quick Analysis tool

Instead of resorting to the Sum button and AutoFill to create totals for a worksheet table, you can use the Totals feature on a Quick Analysis tool to get the job done. A Quick Analysis tool offers a bevy of features for doing anything from adding conditional formatting, charts, pivot tables, and sparklines to your worksheet tables.

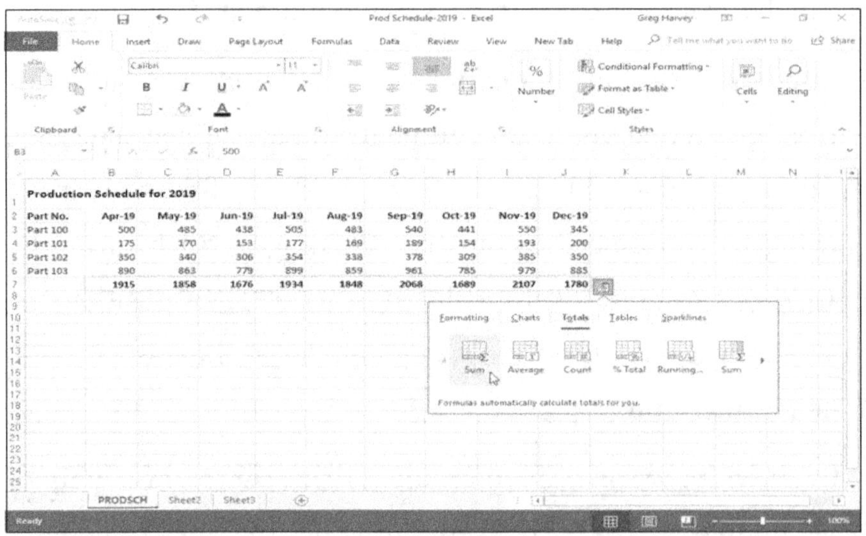

To use a Quick Analysis method, simply pick the cells in the worksheet table, then press a Quick Analysis tool that occurs in the bottom part of the last cell range. While you're doing it, a range of choices emerges under a Quick Analysis method.

To add totals to your selected table data, you first tap the Totals tab. You can then use your mouse or Touch pointer to have Live Preview show you totals in a new row at the bottom by highlighting the Sum or Running Total button (with a spreadsheet containing a Sigma) or in a new column on the right by highlighting the second Sum button (with the spreadsheet with the last column highlighted). To actually add the SUM formulas with the totals to a new row or column, you simply click the Sum or Running Total button of choice.

If you have trouble selecting a Quick Analysis gadget to open its palette for any reason, simply right-click the cell selection and click a Quick Analysis item on its shortcut menu.

Building formulas with computational operators

Many of the simpler formulas that you build require the sole use of Excel's operators, which are the symbols that indicate the kind of operation that is to take place between the cells and/or constants interspersed between them. Excel uses four different kinds of computational operators: arithmetic, comparison, text, and reference.

"Smooth operator"

 If B10 contains the number 15 and C10 contains the number 20, the formula in A10 returns the logical value TRUE. If, however, both cell B10 and C10 contain the value 12, the formula returns the logical value FALSE.

The single text operator (the so-called ampersand) is used in formulas to join together two or more text entries (an operation with the highfalutin' name concatenation). For example, suppose that you enter the following formula in box C2: =A2&B2

If cell A2 contains John and cell B2 contains Smith, the formula returns the new (squashed together) text entry, John Smith. To have the formula insert a space between the first and last names, you have to include the space as part of the concatenation as follows: =A2&" "&B2

You most often use the comparison operators with the IF function when building more complex formulas that perform one type of operation when the IF condition is TRUE and another when it is FALSE. You use the concatenating operator (&) when you need to join text entries that come to you entered in separate cells but that need to be entered in single cells (like the first and last names in separate columns).

Order of operator precedence

When you build a formula that combines different computational operators, Excel follows the set order of operator precedence, as shown in Table 1-2. When you use operators that share the same level of precedence, Excel evaluates each element in the equation by using a strictly left-to-right order.

TABLE 1-2　Natural Order of Operator Precedence in Formulas

Precedence	Operator	Type/Function
1	–	Negation
2	%	Percent
3	^	Exponentiation
4	* and /	Multiplication and Division
5	+ and –	Addition and Subtraction
6	&	Concatenation
7	=, <, >, <=, >=, <>	All Comparison Operators

Suppose that you enter the following formula in cell A4: =B4+C4/D4

Because division (like multiplication) has a higher level of precedence than addition (4 versus 5), Excel evaluates the division between cells C4 and D4 and then adds that result to the value in cell B4. If, for example, cell B4 contains 2, C4 contains 9, and D4 contains 3, Excel would essentially be evaluating this equation in cell A4: =2+9/3

In this example, the calculated result displayed in cell A4 is 5 because the program first performs the division (9/3) that returns the result 3 and then adds it to the 2 to get the final result of 5.

If you had wanted Excel to evaluate this formula in a strictly left-to-right manner, you could get it to do so by enclosing the leftmost operation (the addition between B4 and C4) in a closed pair of parentheses. Parentheses alter the natural order of precedence so that any operation enclosed within a pair is performed before the other operations in the formula, regardless of level in the order. (After that, the natural order is once again used.)

To have Excel perform the addition between the first two terms (B4 and C4) and then divide the result by the third term (cell D4), you modify the original formula by enclosing the addition operation in parentheses as follows: =(B4+C4)/D4

Assuming that cells B4, C4, and D4 still contain the same numbers (2, 9, and 3, respectively), the formula now calculates the result as 3.666667 and returns it to cell A4 (2+9=11 and 11/3=3.66667).

If necessary, you can nest parentheses in your formulas by putting one set of parentheses within another (within another, within another, and so on). When you nest parentheses, Excel performs the calculation in the innermost pair of parentheses first before anything else and then starts performing the operations in the outer parentheses.

Consider the following sample formula: =B5+(C5−D5)/E5

In this formula, the parentheses around the subtraction (C5−D5) ensure that it is the first operation performed. After that, however, the natural order of precedence takes over. So, the result of the subtraction is then divided by the value in E5, and that result is then added to the value in B5. If you want the addition to be performed before the division, you need to nest the first set of parentheses within another set as follows: =(B5+(C5−D5))/E5

In this revised formula, Excel performs the subtraction between the values in C5 and D5, adds the result to the value in cell B5, and then divides that result by the value in cell E5.

Of course, the biggest problem with parentheses is that you have to remember to enter them in pairs. If you forget to balance each set of nested parentheses by having a right parenthesis for every left parenthesis, Excel displays an alert dialog box, informing you that it has located an error in the formula. It will also suggest a correction that would balance the parentheses used in the formula. Although the suggested correction corrects the imbalance in the formula, it, unfortunately, doesn't give you the calculation order that you wanted — and if accepted, the suggested correction would give you what you consider an incorrect result. For this reason, be very careful before you click the Yes button in this kind of Alert dialog box. Do so only when you're certain that the corrected parentheses give you the calculation order that you want. Otherwise, click No and balance the parentheses in the formula by adding the missing parenthesis or parentheses yourself.

Using the Insert Function button

Excel supports a wide variety of built-in functions that you can use when building formulas. Of course, the most popular built-in function is by far the SUM function, which is automatically inserted when you click the Sum command button on the Home tab of the Ribbon. (Keep in mind that you can also use this drop-down button attached to the Sum button to insert the AVERAGE, COUNT, MAX, and MIN functions — see the "When you AutoSum numbers in a spreadsheet" section previously. In this chapter for details.) To use other Excel functions, you can use the Insert Function button on the Formula bar (the one with the fx).

When you click the Insert Function button, Excel displays the Insert Function dialog box, similar to the one shown in Figure 1-4. You can then use its options to find and select the function that you want to use and to define the argument or arguments that the function requires in order to perform its calculation.

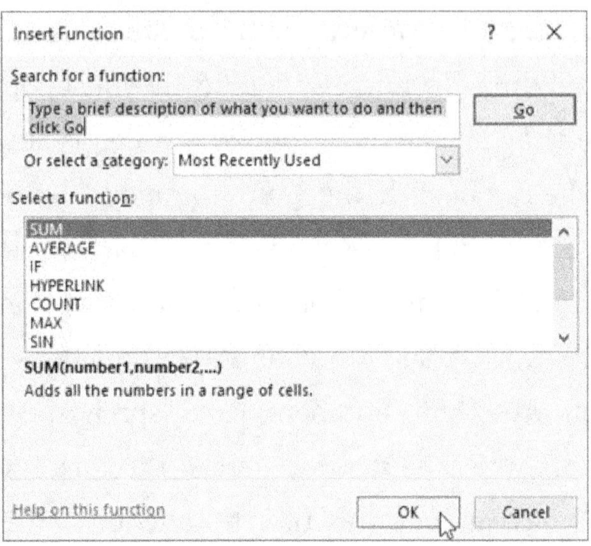

To select the function that you want to use, you can use any of the following methods:

- Click the function name if it's one that you've used lately and is therefore already listed in the Select a Function list box.

- Select the name of the category of the function that you want to use from the Or Select a Category drop-down list box (Most Recently Used is the default category) and then select the function that you want to use in that category from the Select a Function list box.

- Replace the text "Type a brief description of what you want to do and then click Go" in the Search for a Function text box with keywords or a phrase about the type of calculation that you want to do (such as "return on investment"). Click the Go button or press Enter and click the function that you want to use in the Recommended category displayed in the Select a Function

- When selecting the function to use in the Select a Function list box, click the function name to have Excel give you a short description of what the function does, displayed underneath the name of the function with its argument(s) shown in parentheses (referred to as the function's syntax). To get help on using the function, click the Help on This Function link displayed in the lower-left corner of the Insert Function dialog box to open the Help window in its own pane on the right. When you finish reading and/or printing this help topic, click the Close button to close the Help window and return to the Insert Function dialog box.

- You can select the most commonly used types of Excel functions and enter them simply by choosing their names from the drop-down menus attached to their command buttons in the Function Library group of the Formulas tab of the Ribbon. These command buttons include Financial, Logical, Text, Date & Time, Lookup & Reference, and Math & Trig. In addition, you can select functions in the Statistical, Engineering, Cube, Information, Compatibility, and Web categories from continuation menus that appear when you click the

More Functions command button on the Formulas tab. And if you find you need to insert a function in the worksheet that you recently entered into the worksheet, the chances are good that when you click the Recently Used command button, that function will be listed on its dropdown menu for you to select.

- When you click OK after selecting the function that you want to use in the current cell, Excel inserts the function name followed by a closed set of parentheses on the Formula bar. At the same time, the program closes the Insert Function dialog box and then opens the Function Arguments dialog box, similar to the one shown in Figure 1-5. You then use the argument text box or boxes displayed in the Function Arguments dialog box to specify what numbers and other information are to be used when the function calculates its result.

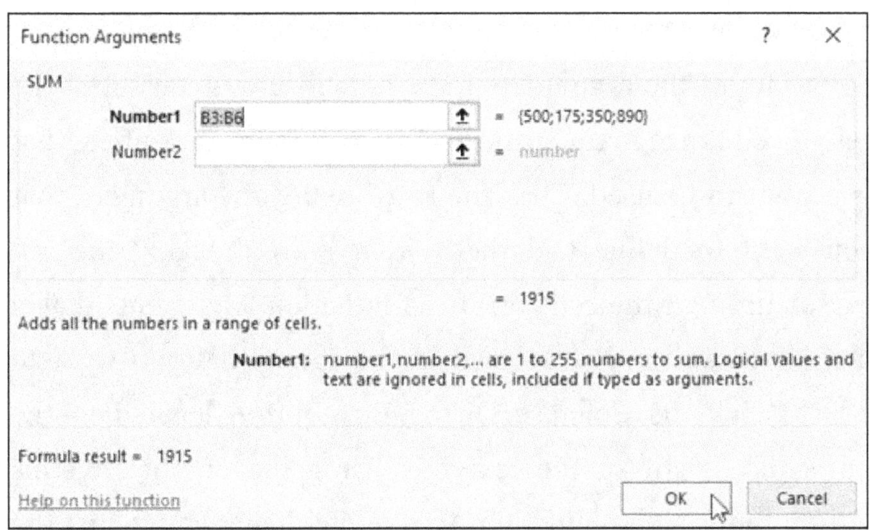

Selecting the arguments for a function in the Function Arguments dialog box.

All functions — even those that don't take any arguments, such as the TODAY function — follow the function name by a closed set of parentheses, as in =TODAY (). If the function requires arguments (and almost all require at least one), these arguments must appear within the parentheses following the function name. When a function requires multiple arguments, such as the DATE function, the various arguments are entered in the required order (as in a year, month, a day for the DATE function) within the parentheses separated by commas, as in DATE (20,7,23).

When you use the text boxes in the Function Arguments dialog box to input the arguments for a function, you can select the cell or cell range in the worksheet that contains the entries that you want to be used. Click the text box for the argument that you want to define and then either start dragging the cell cursor through the cells or, if the Function Arguments dialog box is obscuring the first cell in the range that you want to select, click the Collapse Dialog Box button located to the immediate right of the text box. Dragging or clicking this button reduces the Function Arguments dialog box to just the currently selected argument text box, thus enabling you to drag through the rest of the cells in the range.

If you started dragging without first clicking the Collapse Dialog Box button, Excel automatically expands the Function Arguments dialog box as soon as you release the mouse button. If you clicked the Collapse Dialog Box button, you have to click the Expand Dialog Box button (which replaces the Collapse Dialog Box button located to the right of the argument text box) in order to restore the Function Arguments dialog box to its original size.

As you define arguments for a function in the Function Arguments dialog box, Excel shows you the calculated result following the heading, "Formula result =" near the bottom of the Function Arguments dialog box. When you finish entering the required argument(s) for your function (and any optional arguments that may pertain to your particular calculation), click OK to have Excel close the Function Arguments dialog box and replace the formula in the current cell display with the calculated result.

You can also type the name of the function instead of selecting it from the Insert Function dialog box. When you begin typing a function name after typing an equal sign (=), Excel's AutoComplete feature kicks in by displaying a drop-down menu with the names of all the functions that begin with the character(s) you type. You can then enter the name of the function you want to use by double-clicking its name on this drop-down menu. Excel then enters the function name along with the open parenthesis as in =DATE (so that you can then begin selecting the cell range(s) for the first argument.

For details on how to use different types of built-in functions for your spreadsheets, refer to the following chapters in Book 3 that discuss the use of various categories: Refer to Chapter 2 for information on Logical functions; Chapter 3 for Date and Time functions; Chapter 4 for Financial functions; Chapter 5 for Math and Statistical functions; and Chapter 6 for Lookup, Information, and Text functions.

Copying Formulas

In a spreadsheet that is largely based on calculations, copying equations is among the most common activities. Excel allows copying an initial formula to any spot that needs a certain position a piece of cake because it uses cell comparisons instead of constant numbers (as others should). This is accomplished by the software automatically changing the cell references in the initial formula to match the location of the copies you produce. This is accomplished using a method known as absolute cell addresses, in which the column relations in the cell reference in a formula adjust to their current column location, and the row references adjust to their new row position.

Figures 1-6 and 1-7 illustrate how this works. Figure 1-6, is used the AutoSum button in cell B7 to build the original formula that uses the SUM function that totals the April sales. The formula in cell B7 reads

=SUM (B3:B6)

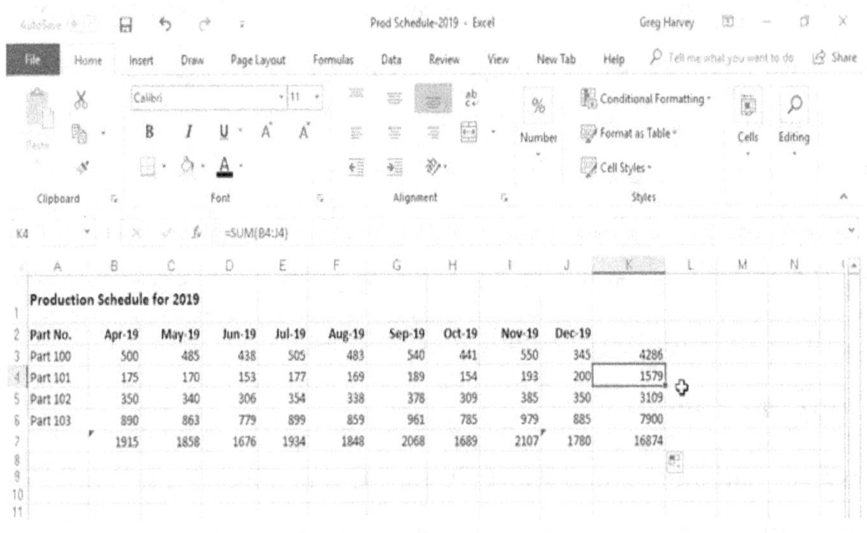

The spreadsheet screenshot shows an Excel window titled "Prod Schedule-2019 - Excel" with the formula bar for cell K4 reading `=SUM(B4:J4)`, and the following data:

Part No.	Apr-19	May-19	Jun-19	Jul-19	Aug-19	Sep-19	Oct-19	Nov-19	Dec-19	
Part 100	500	485	438	505	483	540	441	550	345	4286
Part 101	175	170	153	177	169	189	154	193	200	1579
Part 102	350	340	306	354	338	378	309	385	350	3109
Part 103	890	863	779	899	859	961	785	979	885	7900
	1915	1858	1676	1934	1848	2068	1689	2107	1780	16874

The original formula is copied with the fill handle across the last row of the spreadsheet table.

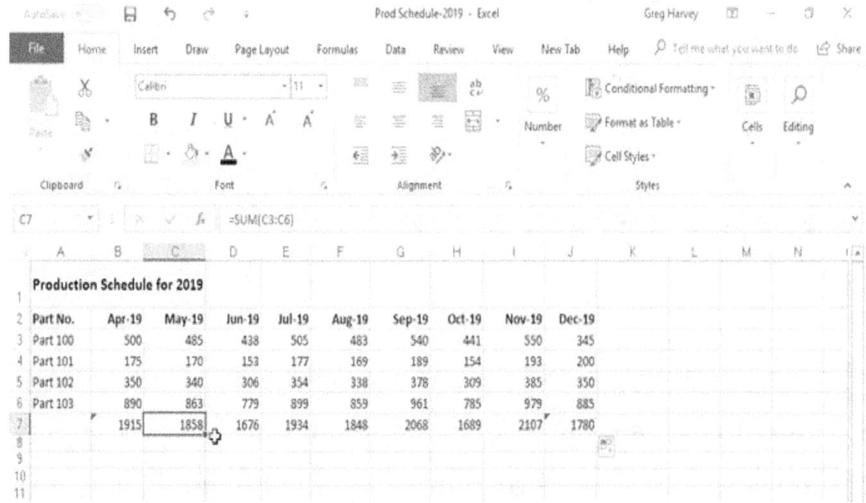

The original formula is copied with the fill handle down the last column of the data table.

I then used the AutoFill feature to copy this formula by dragging the fill handle to include the cell range B7:J7. (Copying the formula with the cut-and-paste method would work just as well, although it's a little more work.) Note in the cell range C7:J7 that Excel did not copy the original formula to the other cells verbatim. (Otherwise, each of the copied formulas would return the same result, 1915, as the original in cell B7.) If you look at the Formula bar in Figure 1-5, you see that the copy of the original formula in cell C7 reads

=SUM (C3:C6)

In this copy, Excel adjusted the column reference of the range being summed from B to C to suit the new position of the copy. Figure 1-7 shows how this works when copying an original

formula in the other direction, this time down a column. For this figure, I used the AutoSum button to create a SUM formula that totals all the monthly sales for Part 100 in row 3. The formula in cell K3 reads

=SUM (B3:J3)

You can then use the fill handle to copy this formula down the last column of the table to include the cell range by positioning the cell cursor in K3 and then dragging the fill handle down to select K3:K7. If you were to then position the cell cursor in cell K4, you would see on the Formula bar that when Excel copied the original formula in cell K3 down to cell K4, it automatically adjusted the row reference to suit its new position so that the formula in cell K4 reads

=SUM (B4:J4)

Although at first glance it appears that Excel isn't making exact copies of the original formula when it uses the relative cell addressing, that isn't technically true. Although the cell column references in the first example in Figure 1-6 and the row references in the second example in Figure 1-7 appear to be adjusted to suit the new column and row position when you view the worksheet by using the R1C1 cell notation system, you'd actually see that, in R1C1 notation (unlike the default A1 system), each and every copy of the original formula is exactly the same.

For example, the original formula that I input into cell B7 (known as cell R7C2 in the R1C1 system) to sum the April sales for all the different part numbers reads as follows when you switch to R1C1 notation:

=SUM (R [−4]C: R[−1]C)

In this notation, the SUM formula is more difficult to decipher, so I will explain and then translate it for you. In R1C1 notation, the cell range in the SUM argument is expressed in terms completely relative to the position of the cell containing the formula. The row portion of the cell range expresses how many rows above or below the one with the formula the rows are. (Negative integers indicate rows above, whereas positive integers indicate rows below.) The column portion of the cell range in the SUM argument expresses how many columns to the left or right of the one with the formula the columns are. (Positive integers indicate columns to the right, and negative integers indicate columns to the left.) When a column or row in the cell range is not followed by an integer in square brackets, this means that there is no change in the column or row.

Armed with this information, my translation R1C1 form of this formula may just make sense; it says, "sum the values in the range of the cells that is four rows (R[−4]) above the current cell in the same column (C) down through the cell that is just one row (R[−1]) above the current cell in the same column (C)."

When this original formula is copied over to the columns in the rest of the table, it doesn't need to be changed because each copy of the formula performs this exact calculation (when expressed in such relative terms).

The original formula in Figure 1-7 that I entered into cell K3 and copied down to cell K6 appears as follows when you switch over to the R1C1 notation:

=SUM (RC [−9]: RC [−1])

It says, "sum the range of values in the cell nine columns to the left (C [−9]) in the same row through the cell that is one column to the left (C [−1]) in the same row." This is exactly what all the copies of this formula in the rows below do so that when Excel copies this formula, it doesn't change.

You can use the R1C1 notation to check that you've copied all the formulas in a spreadsheet table correctly. Just switch to the R1C1 system by clicking the R1C1 Reference Style check box in the Working with Formulas section on the Formulas tab of the Excel Options dialog box (File ⇨ Options ⇨ Formulas). Then move the cell Using an absolute address in the formula to calculate the monthly percentage of the total.

Cursor through all the cells with copied formulas in the table. When R1C1 notation is in effect, all copies of an original formula across an entire row or down an entire column of the table

should be identical when displayed on the Formula bar as you make their cells current.

Absolute references

Most of the time, relative cell references are exactly what you need in the formulas that you build, thus allowing Excel to adjust the row and/or column references as required in the copies that you make. You will encounter some circumstances, however, where Excel should not adjust one or more parts of the cell reference in the copied formula. This occurs, for example, whenever you want to use a cell value as a constant in all the copies that you make of a formula.

Figure 1-8 illustrates just such a situation. In this situation, you want to build a formula in cell B9 that calculates what percentage April's part production total (B7) is of the total nine-month production (cell K7). Normally, you would create the following formula in cell B9 with all its relative cell references:

=B7/K7

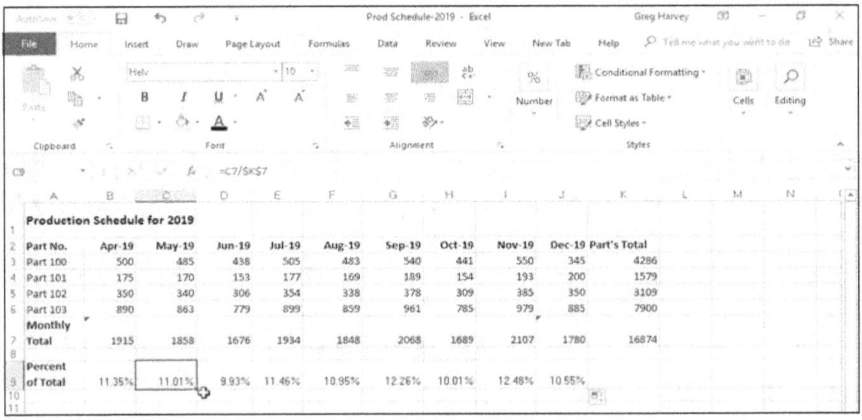
Prod Schedule-2019 - Excel
Greg Harvey
File
Home
Insert
Draw
Page Layout
Formulas
Data
Review
View
New Tab
Help
Share
Conditional Formatting
Format as Table
Cell Styles
Number
Cells
Editing
Clipboard
Font
Alignment
Styles
C9
=C7/$K$7
Production Schedule for 2019
Part No. Apr-19 May-19 Jun-19 Jul-19 Aug-19 Sep-19 Oct-19 Nov-19 Dec-19 Part's Total
Part 100 500 485 438 505 483 540 441 550 345 4286
Part 101 175 170 153 177 169 189 154 193 200 1579
Part 102 350 340 306 354 338 378 309 385 350 3109
Part 103 890 863 779 899 859 961 785 979 885 7900
Monthly Total 1915 1858 1676 1934 1848 2068 1689 2107 1780 16874
Percent of Total 11.35% 11.01% 9.93% 11.46% 10.95% 12.26% 10.01% 12.48% 10.55%

However, because you want to copy this formula across to the range C9:J9 to calculate the percentages for the eight months (May through December), you need to alter the relative cell references in the last part of the formula in cell K7 so that this cell reference with the nine-month production total remains unchanged in all your copies.

You can start to understand the problem caused by adjusting a relative cell reference that should remain unchanged by just thinking about copying the original formula from cell B9 to C9 to calculate the percentage for May. In this cell, you want the following formula that divides the May production total in cell C7 by the nine-month total in cell K7: =C7/K7

However, if you don't indicate otherwise, Excel adjusts both parts of the formula in the copies so that C9 incorrectly contains the following formula: =C7/L7

Because cell L7 is currently blank and blank cells have the equivalent of the value 0, this formula returns the #DIV/0! Formula error as a result, thus indicating that Excel can't properly perform this arithmetic operation.

To indicate that you don't want a particular cell reference (such as cell K7 in the example) to be adjusted in the copies that you make of a formula, you change the cell reference from a relative cell reference to an absolute cell reference. In the A1 system of cell references, an absolute cell reference contains dollar signs before the column letter and the row number, as in $K$7. In the R1C1 notation, you simply list the actual row and column number in the cell reference, as in R7C11, without placing the row and column numbers in square brackets.

If you realize that you need to convert a relative cell reference to an absolute reference as you're building the original formula, you can convert the relative reference to absolute by selecting the cell and then pressing F4. To get an idea of how this works, follow along with these steps for creating the correct formula =B7/$K$7 in cell B9:

1. Click cell B9 to make it active.

2. Type = to start the formula; then click cell B7 and type / (the sign for division).

3. The Formula bar now reads =B7/.

4. Click K7 to select this cell and add it to the formula.

5. The Formula bar now reads =B7/K7.

6. Press F4 once to change the cell reference from relative (K7) to absolute ($K$7).

7. The Formula bar now reads =B7/$K$7. You're now ready to enter the formula and then make the copies.

8. Click the Enter button on the Formula bar and then drag the fill handle to cell J9 before you release the mouse button.

Like it or not, you won't always anticipate the need for an absolute value until after you've built the formula and copied it to a range. When this happens, you have to edit the original formula, change the relative reference to absolute, and then make the copies again.

When editing the cell reference in the formula, you can change its reference by positioning the insertion point anywhere in its address and then pressing F4. You can also do this by inserting dollar signs in front of the column letter(s) and row number when editing the formula, although doing that isn't nearly as easy as pressing F4.

You can make an exact copy of the formula in another cell without using absolute references. To do this, make the cell with the formula that you want to copy the active one, use the I-beam pointer to select the entire formula in the Formula bar by dragging through it, and then click the Copy command button on the Home tab of the Ribbon (or press Ctrl+C). Next, click the Cancel button to deactivate the Formula bar, select the cell where you want the exact copy to appear, and then click the Paste command button on the Home tab (or press Ctrl+V). Excel then pastes an exact duplicate of the original formula into the active cell without adjusting any of its cell references (even if they are all relative cell references).

Keep in mind when using the sum options on the Totals tab of a Quick Analysis tool's palette (see "Totals and sums with a Quick Analysis tool" earlier in this chapter for details) that all the cell references in the total and sum formulas that Excel creates are relative references.

If you're building the formula that requires an absolute or some sort of mixed cell reference (see the following section) on a touchscreen device and using the Touch keyboard with no access to function keys, you need to add the required dollar sign(s) into the formula on the Formula bar by using the dollar sign ($) key on the Touch keyboard. To access the dollar sign key, tap the Numeric key (&123) to switch the Touch keyboard out of the QWERTY letter arrangement.

A mixed bag of references

Some formulas don't require you to change the entire cell reference from relative to absolute in order to copy them correctly. In some situations, you need to indicate only that the column letter or the row number remains unchanged in all copies of the original formula. A cell reference that is part relative and part absolute is called a mixed cell reference.

In the A1 notation, a mixed cell reference has a dollar sign just in front of the column letter or row number that should not be adjusted in the copies. For example, $C10 adjusts row 10 in copies down the rows but leaves column C unchanged in all copies across columns to its right. Another example is C$10, which adjusts column C in copies to columns to the right but leaves row 10 unchanged in all copies down the rows.

To change the cell reference that you select in a formula (by clicking the flashing insertion point somewhere in its column letter and row number) from relative to mixed, continue to press F4 until the type of mixed reference appears on the Formula bar. When the Formula bar is active, and the insertion point is somewhere in the cell reference (either when building or editing the formula), pressing F4 cycles through each cell-reference possibility in the following order:

- The first time you press F4, Excel changes the relative cell reference to absolute (C10 to $C$10).

- The second time you press F4, Excel changes the absolute reference to a mixed reference where the column is relative, and the row is absolute ($C$10

- The third time you select the Reference command, Excel changes the mixed reference where the column is relative, and the row is absolute to a mixed reference where the row is relative, and the column is absolute (C$10 to $C10).

- The fourth time you press F4, Excel changes the mixed reference where the row is relative, and the column is absolute back to a relative reference ($C10 to C10).

As noted previously in this chapter, many spreadsheet tables use an original formula that you copy to adjacent cells by using relative cell references (sometimes referred to as a one-to-many copy). In some cases, you can build the original formula so that Excel performs the desired calculation not only in the active cell but also in all the other cells to which you would normally copy the formula.

You do this by creating an array formula. An array formula is a special formula that operates on a range of values. If a cell range supplies this range (as is often the case), it is referred to as an array range. If this range is supplied by a list of numerical values, they are known as an array constant.

Although the array concept may seem foreign at first, you are really quite familiar with arrays because the column-and-row structure of the Excel worksheet grid naturally organizes your data ranges into one-dimensional and two-dimensional arrays. (1-D arrays take up a single row or column, whereas 2-D arrays take up multiple rows and columns.)

Figure 1-9 illustrates a couple of two-dimensional arrays with numerical entries of two different sizes. The first array is a 3 x 2 array in the cell range B2:C4. This array is a 3 x 2 array because it occupies three rows and two columns. The second array is a 2 x 3 array in the cell range F2:H3. This array is a 2 x 3 array because it uses two rows and three columns.

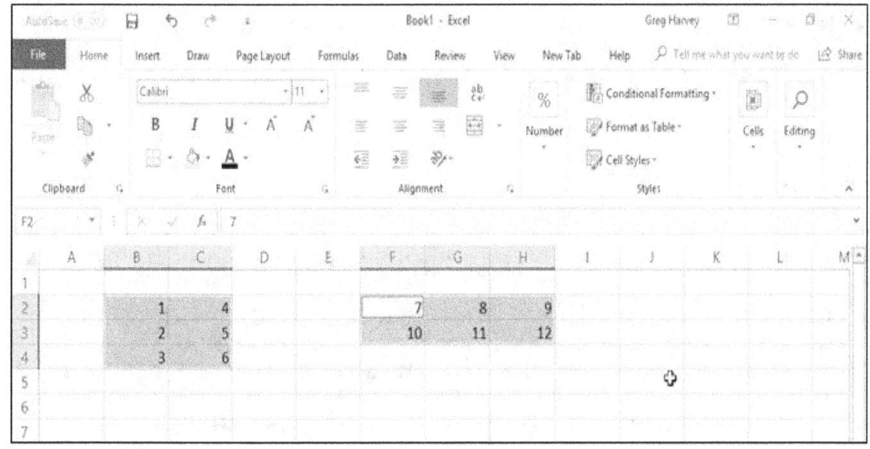

Worksheet with two different sizes of arrays.

If you were to list the values in the first 3 x 2 array as an array constant in a formula, they would appear as follows:

{1,4;2,5;3,6}

Several things in this list are noteworthy. First, the array constant is enclosed in a pair of braces ({}). Second, columns within each row are separated by commas (,) and rows within the array are separated by semicolons (;). Third, the constants in the array are listed across each row and then down each column and not down each column and across each row.

The second 2 x 3 array expressed as an array constant appears as follows:

{7,8,9;10,11,12}

Note again that you list the values across each row and then down each column, separating the values in different columns with commas and the values in different rows with a semicolon.

The use of array formulas can significantly reduce the amount of formula copying that you have to do in a worksheet by producing multiple results throughout the array range in a single operation. In addition, array formulas use less computer memory than standard formulas copied in a range. This can be important when creating a large worksheet with many tables because it may mean the difference between fitting all your calculations on one worksheet and having to split your model into several worksheet files.

Editing an array formula

Editing array formulas differ somewhat from editing normal formulas. In editing an array range, you must treat the range as a single unit and edit it in one operation (corresponding to the way in which the array formula was entered). This means that you can't edit, clear, move, insert, or delete individual cells in the array range. If you try, Excel will display an Alert dialog box stating, "You cannot change part of an array."

To edit the contents of an array formula, select a cell in the array range and then activate Edit mode by clicking the formula or the Formula bar or pressing F2. When you do this, Excel displays the contents of the array formula without the customary braces. The program also outlines the ranges referred to in the array formula in the cells of the worksheet in different colors that match those assigned to the range

addresses in the edited formula on the Formula bar. After you make your changes to the formula contents, you must remember to press Ctrl+Shift+Enter to enter your changes and have Excel enclose the array formula in braces once again.

If you want to convert the results in an array range to their calculated values, select the array range and click the Copy button on the Ribbon's Home tab or press Ctrl+C. Then, without changing the selection, click the Paste Values option from the Paste button's drop-down menu (or press Alt+HVV). As soon as you convert an array range to its calculated values, Excel no longer treats the cell range as an array.

Range Names in Formulas

Thus far, all the example formulas in this chapter have used a combination of numerical constants and cell references (both relative and absolute and using the A1 and R1C1 notation). Although cell references provide a convenient method for pointing out the cell location in the worksheet grid, they are not at all descriptive of their function when used in formulas. Fortunately, Excel makes it easy to assign descriptive names to the cells, cell ranges, constants, and even formulas that make their function in the worksheet much more understandable.

To get an idea of how names can help to document the purpose of a formula, consider the following formula for computing the sale price of an item that uses standard cell references:

=B4*B2

Now consider the following formula that performs the same calculation but, this time, with the use of range names:

=Retail Price*Discount Rate

Obviously, the function of the second formula is much more comprehensible, not only to you as the creator of the worksheet but also to anyone else who has to use it.

Range names are extremely useful not only for documenting the function of the formulas in your worksheet but also for finding and selecting cell ranges quickly and easily. This is especially helpful in a large worksheet that you aren't very familiar with or only use intermittently. After you assign a name to a cell range, you can locate and select all the cells in that range with the Go To dialog box.

Simply click the Go To option from the Find & Select button's drop-down menu on the Home tab of the Ribbon (or press Ctrl+G or F5). Then double-click the range name in the Go-To list box, or click the range name and click OK or press Enter. Excel then selects the entire range and, if necessary, shifts the worksheet display so that you can see the first cell in that range on the screen.

If you're using Excel 2019 on a Windows device such as a tablet without the benefit of a keyboard or mouse, you will definitely find it to your advantage to assigning range names to often-used cell ranges in your spreadsheets. That way, you can go to and

select these ranges simply by tapping the Name box drop-down button followed by the range name. That's so much faster and easier than manually finding and selecting the range with your finger or stylus.

Defining range names

You can define a name for the selected cell range or nonadjacent selection by typing its range name into the Name box on the Formula bar and then pressing Enter. You can also name a cell, cell range, or nonadjacent selection by clicking the Define Name command button on the Ribbon's Formulas tab or by pressing Alt+MMD. Excel then opens the New Name dialog box, where you can input the selection's range name in the Name text box.

If Excel can identify a label in the cell immediately above or to the left of the active one, the program inserts this label as the suggested name in the Name text box. The program also displays the scope of the range name in the Scope drop-down list box and the cell reference of the active cell or the range address of the range or nonadjacent selection that is currently marked (by using absolute references) in the Refers To text box below. You can do the following:

- To change the scope from the entire workbook to a particular worksheet in the workbook so that the range name is only recognized on that sheet, select the sheet's name from the Scope drop-down list.

- To change the cell, range the name refers to, select the cells in the worksheet.

- Remember that you can collapse the New Name dialog box to the Refers To text box by clicking its Collapse button.)

To accept the suggested or edited name, scope, and cell selection, click the OK button, shown in Figure 1-12.

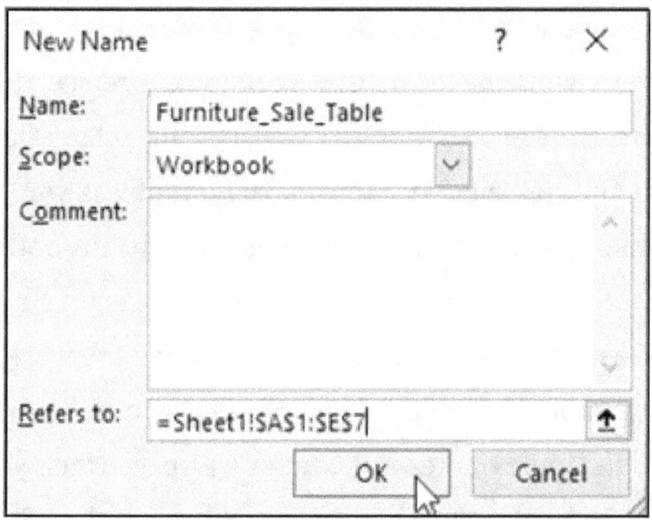

When naming a range in the Name text box of the New Name dialog box, you need to follow the same naming conventions as to when defining a name in the Name box on the Formula bar. Basically, this means that the name must begin with a letter rather than a number, contain no spaces, and not duplicate any other name in the workbook.

Adding a new range name in the New Name dialog box.

If you want to assign the same range name to similar ranges on different worksheets in the workbook, preface the range name with the sheet name followed by an exclamation point and then the descriptive name. For example, if you want to give the name Costs to the cell range A2:A10 on both Sheet1 and Sheet2, you name the range Sheet1! Costs on Sheet1 and Sheet2! Costs on Sheet2. If you have renamed the worksheet to something more descriptive than Sheet1, you need to enclose the name in single quotes if it contains a space when you enter the range. For example, if you rename Sheet1 to Inc. Statement 19, you enter the range name including the worksheet reference for the Costs cell range as follows:

'Inc. Statement 19'! Costs

When you preface a range name with the sheet name as shown in this example, you don't have to use the sheet name part of the range name in the formulas that you create on the same worksheet. In other words, if you create a SUM formula that totals the values in the 'Inc. Statement 16'! Costs range somewhere on the Inc. Statement 16 worksheet; you can enter the formulas as follows:

=SUM(Costs)

However, if you were to create this formula on any other worksheet in the workbook, you would have to include the full range name in the formula, as in =SUM ('Inc. Statement 16'! Costs)

Naming constants and formulas

In addition to naming cells in your worksheet, you can also assign range names to the constants and formulas that you use often. For example, if you are creating a spreadsheet table that calculates sales prices, you can assign the discount percentage rate to the range name discount rate. Then, you can supply this range name as a constant in any formula that calculates the sale discount used in determining the sale price for the merchandise.

For example, to assign a constant value of 15% to the range name discount rate, you open the New Name dialog box and then type discount rate in the Name text box and =15% as the discount rate in the Refers To text box before clicking OK. After assigning this constant percentage rate to the range name discount_ rate in this manner, you can apply it to any formula by typing or pasting in the name (see the "Using names in building formulas" section that follows in this chapter for details).

In addition to naming constants, you can also give a range name to a formula that you use repeatedly. When building a formula in the Refers To text box of the New Name dialog box (Alt+MMD), keep in mind that Excel automatically applies absolute references to any cells that you point to in the worksheet. If you want to create a formula with relative cell references that Excel adjusts when you enter or paste the range name in a new cell, you must press F4 to convert the current cell reference to relative or type in the cell address without dollar signs.

When creating the constant in the New Name dialog box, don't change the Scope setting from Workbook to a particular sheet in the workbook unless you're positive that you'll never need to use that constant in a formula on any other worksheet. If you limit the scope to a particular worksheet, Excel 2019 does not let you use the range name in a formula on any other worksheet (you'll get the #NAME? error), and Scope is the one aspect you can't change when editing a range name via the Name Manager.

Using names in building formulas

After you assign a name to a cell or cell range in your worksheet, you can then click the range name from the Use in Formula button's drop-down menu on the Ribbon's Formulas tab to paste it into the formulas that you build (Alt+MS).

For example, in the sample Autumn 2016 Furniture Sale table shown in Figure 1-13, after assigning the discount rate of 15% to the range name, discount rate, you can create the formulas that calculate the amount of the sale discount. To do this, you multiply the retail price of each item by the discount rate constant using the Use in Formula command button by following these steps:

1. Make cell D3 active.

2. Type = (equal sign) to start the formula.

3. Click cell C3 to select the retail price for the first item and then type * (asterisk).

4. The formula on the Formula bar now reads, =C3*.

5. Click the Use in Formula button on the FORMULAS tab or press Alt+MS.

6. This action opens the drop-down menu on the Use in Formula button on which you can select the discount rate range name.

7. Choose the name discount rate from the Use in Formula button's drop-down menu.

8. The formula now reads =C3*discount rate on the Formula bar.

9. Click the Enter button on the Formula bar to input the formula in cell D3.

10. Now, all that remains is to copy the original formula down column D.

11. Drag the fill handle in cell D3 down to cell D7 and release the mouse button to copy the formula and calculate the discount for the entire table.

Pasting the range name for the discount rate constant into a formula.

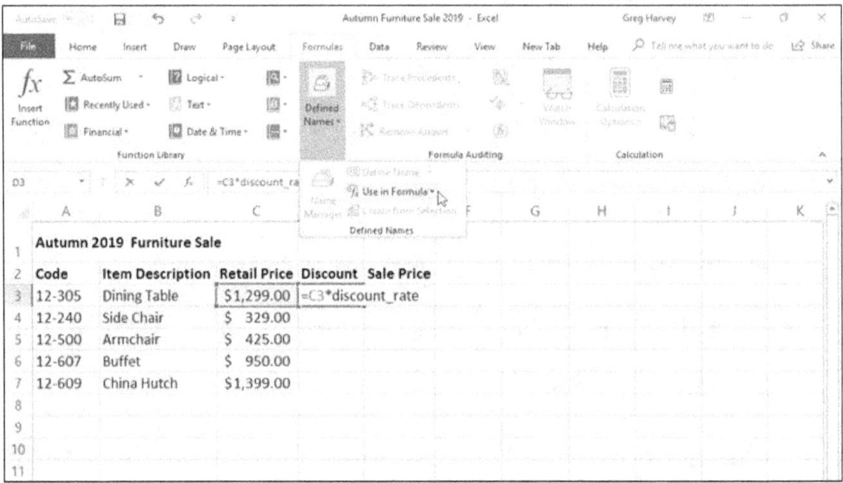

Creating names from column and row headings

You can use the Create from Selection command button on the Formulas tab of the Ribbon to assign existing column and row headings in a table of data to the cells in that table. When using this command button, you can have Excel assign the labels used as column headings in the top or bottom row of the table, the labels used as row headings in the leftmost or rightmost column, or even a combination of these headings.

For example, the sample worksheet in Figure 1-14 illustrates a typical table layout that uses column headings in the top row of the table and row headings in the first column of the table. You can assign these labels to the cells in the table by using the Create from Selection command button as follows:

1. Select the cells in the table, including those with the column and row labels that you want to use as range names.

For the example shown in Figure 1-14, you select the range B2:E7.

2. Click the Create from Selection command button on the Formulas tab or press Alt+MC.

This action opens the Create Names from Selection dialog box that contains four checkboxes: Top Row, Left Column, Bottom Row, and Right Column. The program selects the check box or boxes in this dialog box based on the arrangement of the labels in your table. In the example shown in Figure 1-14, Excel selects both the Top Row and Left Column checkboxes because the table contains both column headings in the top row and row headings in the left column.

3. After selecting (or deselecting) the appropriate Create Names In checkboxes, click the OK button to assign the range names to your table.

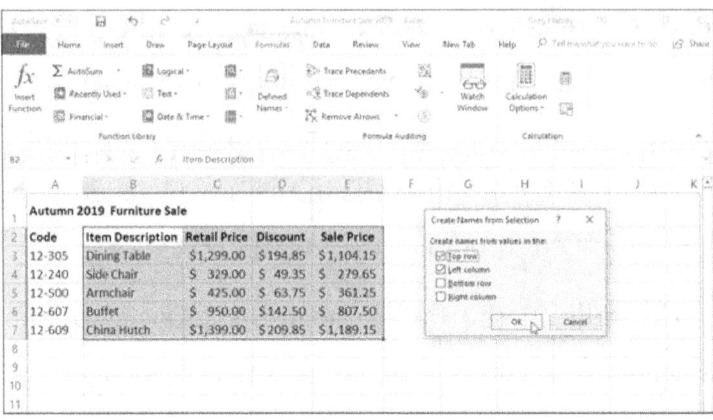

Creating range names from the row and column headings in a spreadsheet table.

Note that when you select both the Top Row and Left Column checkboxes in the Create Names from Selection dialog box, Excel assigns the label in the cell in the upper-left corner of the table to the entire range of values in the table (one row down and one column to the right).

In the example illustrated in Figure 1-14, Excel assigns the name Item Description (the heading for column B) to the cell range C3:E7. Similarly, the program assigns the column headings to the appropriate data in the table in the rows below and assigns the row headings to the data in the appropriate columns to the right so that the name Retail Price is assigned to the cell range C3:C7 and the name China Hutch is assigned to the cell range C7:E7.

Controlling Formula Recalculation

Normally, Excel recalculates your worksheet automatically as soon you change any entries, formulas, or names on which your formulas depend. This system works fine as long as the worksheet is not too large or doesn't contain tables whose formulas depend on several values.

When Excel does calculate your worksheet, the program recalculates only those cells that are affected by the change that you've made. Nevertheless, in a complex worksheet that

contains many formulas, recalculation may take several seconds (during which time, the pointer will change to an hourglass, and the word "Recalculation" followed by the number of cells left to be recalculated will appear on the left side of the Formula bar).

Because Excel recalculates dependent formulas in the background, you can always interrupt this process and make a cell entry or click a command even when the pointer assumes the hourglass shape during the recalculation process. As soon as you stop making entries or selecting commands, Excel resumes recalculating the worksheet.

To control when Excel calculates your worksheet, you click the Calculation Options button on the Formulas tab of the Ribbon and then click the Manual option button or press Alt+MXM. After switching to manual recalculation, when you make a change in a value, formula, or name that would usually cause Excel to recalculate the worksheet, the program displays the message "Calculate" on the Status bar.

When you're ready to have Excel recalculate the worksheet, you then click the Calculate Now (F9) command button (the one with a picture of the handheld calculator) on the Ribbon's FORMULAS tab or press F9 or Ctrl+=. This tells the program to recalculate all dependent formulas and open charts and makes the Calculate status indicator disappear from the Status bar.

After switching to manual recalculation, Excel still automatically recalculates the worksheet whenever you save the file. When you are working with a really large and complex worksheet, recalculating the worksheet each time you want to save your changes can make this process quite time-consuming. If you need to save the worksheet without first updating dependent formulas and charts, you need to deselect the Recalculate Workbook before the Saving check box in the Calculation Options section of the Formulas tab of the Excel Options dialog box (File ⇨ Options ⇨ Formulas or Alt+FTF).

If your worksheet contains data tables used to perform what-if analyses, switch from Automatic to Automatic except Data Tables recalculation by choosing Automatic Except for Data Tables from the Options button's drop-down menu on the Formulas tab or pressing Alt+MXE. Doing so enables you to change a number of variables in the what-if formulas before having Excel recalculate the data table. Automatic, Automatic Except Data Tables and Manual are by no means the only calculation options available in Excel.

Circular References

A circular reference in an equation is one that depends, directly or indirectly, on its own value. The most common type of circular reference occurs when you mistakenly refer in the formula to the cell in which you're building the formula itself.

For example, suppose that cell B10 is active when you build this formula:

=A10+B10

As soon as you click the Enter button on the Formula bar or press Enter or an arrow key to insert this equation in cell B10 (assuming the program is in Automatic recalculation mode), Excel displays an alert dialog box, stating that it cannot calculate the formula due to the circular reference.

If you then press Enter or click OK to close this Alert dialog box, an Excel Help window appears containing general information about circular references in two sections: Locate and Remove a Circular Reference and Make a Circular Reference Work by Changing the Number of Times Microsoft Excel Iterates Formulas.

When you close this Excel Help window by clicking its Close button, Excel inserts 0 in the cell with the circular reference, and the Circular Reference status indicator followed by the cell address with the circular reference appears on the Status bar.

Some circular references are solvable by increasing the number of times they are recalculated (each recalculation bringing you closer and closer to the desired result), whereas others are not (for no amount of recalculating brings them closer to any resolution) and need to be removed from the spreadsheet.

The formula in cell B10 is an example of a circular reference that Excel is unable to resolve because the formula's calculation depends directly on the formula's result. Each time the formula returns a new result, this result is fed into the formula, thus creating a new result to be fed back into the formula. Because this type of circular reference sets up an endless loop that continuously requires recalculating and can never be resolved, you need to fix the formula reference or remove the formula from the spreadsheet.

Figure 1-17 illustrates the classic example of a circular reference, which ultimately can be resolved. Here, you have an income statement that includes bonuses equal to 20 percent of the net earnings entered as an expense in cell B15 with the formula

$$=-B21*20\%$$

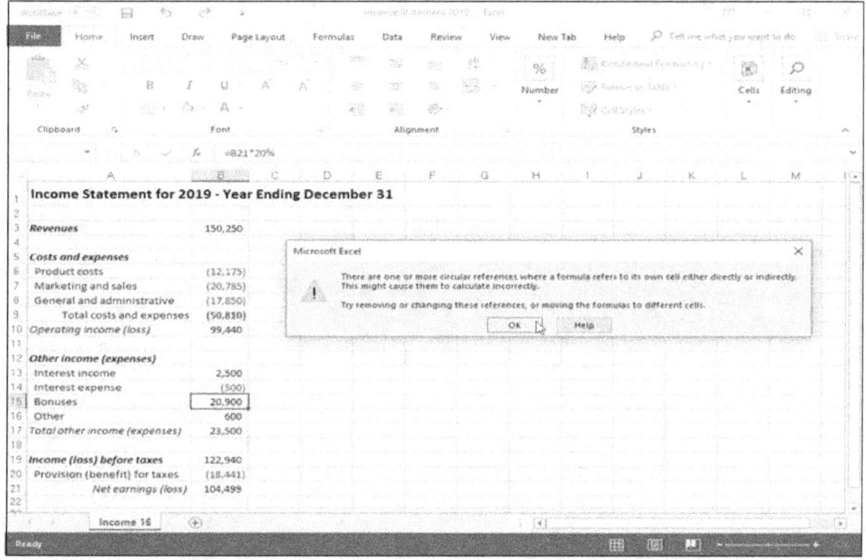

Income statement with a resolvable circular reference.

This formula contains a circular reference because it refers to the value in B21, which itself indirectly depends on the number of bonuses (the bonuses being accounted for as an expense in the very worksheet formulas that determine the number of net earnings in cell B21).

To resolve the circular reference in cell B15 and calculate the bonuses based on net earnings in B21, you simply need to click the Enable Iterative Calculation check box in the Calculation Options section of the Formulas tab in the Excel Options dialog box (File ⇨ Options ⇨ Formulas or Alt+FTF). However, if manual recalculation is selected, you must click the Calculate Now (F9) command button on the Formulas tab of the Ribbon or press F9 or Ctrl+= as well.

Conclusion

Excel has a computer language called VBA [Visual Basic for Applications] associated with it. Really good exponents of Excel use VBA all the time. If you wish to master it, you must know the basics of formulas and functions inside and out.

This book has thoroughly covered many of those basics. Before you proceed further with formulas and functions, you must master the material in the book to the extent that you can do the problems in every chapter.

Once you have mastered the material in this book, you are ready for all the other things that can be done with EXCEL.